holy hell

a case against eternal damnation

derek ryan kubilus

william b. eerdmans publishing company
grand rapids, michigan

Wm. B. Eerdmans Publishing Co.
4035 Park East Court SE, Grand Rapids, Michigan 49546
www.eerdmans.com

Book design by Lydia Hall

Printed in the United States of America

30 29 28 27 26 25 24   1 2 3 4 5 6 7

ISBN 978-0-8028-8317-9

Library of Congress Cataloging-in-Publication Data

A catalog record for this book is available from the Library of
Congress.

Content warning: This book is about the worst thing that humankind has ever attempted to imagine: a hell of eternal torment. That
means these pages are full of some really tough stuff: torture, abuse,
rape, and violence of all kinds. Suicide, racism, and misogyny will all
be discussed at length. Please take care if any of this might present a
challenge to your emotional or psychological well-being.

Unless otherwise indicated, Scripture quotations are from the New
Revised Standard Version, Updated Edition.

For Maggie

contents

acknowledgments

One of the themes of this book is that on some level, we are connected. I believe that God created human life as a kind of web, whereby we are all tied to one another, in some way, both in this life and in the hereafter. That means there is nothing we do, nothing we make, and nothing we accomplish all by ourselves.

To that end, I want to thank the people who made this work possible.

To my wife, Maggie: Thank you for all your support and encouragement, for talking me through the revelation that led to this book, for having the patience to deal with all my emotions as I wrote and doubted and dreamed, and for being my first and most important editor. You have tamed me, and because of that, truly, the sun shines on my life.

To my family, especially my parents, thank you for giving me all the support I need. I could not be the preacher or the writer or even the person I am today without you.

To my friends, especially Christopher Adams, Toby James, and Rich Bryant, thank you for your encouragement, for asking me how the book was coming, and for being excited that I was doing this.

To Mike Hale, Mark Gorsuch, Rev. Allan Bevere, Rev. Stephanie Woods, Rev. Becky Weamer, and Ben Emmert-Aronson, thank you for taking the time to read and offer comments. Some of you were involved at the very beginning, and if not for your willingness to read what I had written, I might not have believed that anyone else would have read it.

And I want to thank the churches that I served while I was writing, the People Called Methodist at Uniontown United Methodist Church and Ashland First United Methodist Church. Thank you for praying for me, for encouraging me, for being excited for me, and for putting up with your vicar having a project on the side. To Uniontown, you guys were there when it all started, and our class on heaven and hell helped me think through the subject matter of this book in a deep and meaningful way. I'll remember that for the rest of my life.

haunted by hell

We are each our own devil, and we make this world
our hell.

—Oscar Wilde, *The Duchess of Padua*

Believe it or not, as a preacher, I don't really talk that much
about the afterlife. I don't give altar calls or launch any "cru-
sades" for lost souls. I can't remember the last time I mused from
the pulpit about the "golden streets of heaven" or warned my congregation to beware the fiery wrath of hell. I know that it might
seem like a dereliction of duty to those who imagine that the
primary function of every sermon is to save souls from eternal
damnation, but in actual day-to-day ministry, it doesn't really
come up that much.

In the midst of leading worship and prayer services, officiating
at weddings and baptisms, visiting people in the hospital, over-
seeing ministry, and teaching Bible study (not to mention all the
paperwork), heaven and hell just fade into the background somewhere. Folks don't often come to me asking about how to go to
heaven or how to avoid going to hell. Instead, they mostly want to
know about things that concern their life on this side of the grave,
such as how they can heal their relationships, how to pray, how

to deal with a family member's addiction, or how to live with the grief of losing a loved one. The life of an ordained pastor is rich and varied such that no two days are ever the same (and that's something I love about it), but if you were to ask me to rank all the duties of my job, "getting my congregation to heaven" and "saving souls from the fires of hell" wouldn't even break the top ten.

But still, every once in a while conversations pop up that remind me that heaven and hell are always in the background, just offshore, the gravity of their respective hopes and fears pulling on the spiritual tides of my congregation—and sometimes the waves break against their lives.

tormented by hell

I had a woman in one of my Bible studies, an ex-Catholic, who had been haunted for years by the idea that her stillborn son found his way to someplace called limbo, a gray nothingness between heaven and hell where, as she had been told by her priest (quite wrongly, according to Catholic doctrine), all unbaptized children spend eternity.

A man from my community who was totally uninterested in church called me late one night. His firstborn son had just been killed in a car accident. He wanted me to do the funeral because he knew me and respected me, and surely I would "do everything right" to get his "boy to heaven."

Finally, there are those who are utterly convinced that they are going to hell. They usually assume that they have some terrible, unforgivable sin in the past and that their destiny is inexorably fixed in a hell of eternal torment. No amount of pastoral reassurance or declarations of God's forgiveness will ever convince them otherwise. I've been genuinely surprised to learn over the years that at least one person in every congregation I have ever served *knew* beyond all shadow of a doubt that they were already sentenced to torturous damnation. I'm not sure why such folks still come to church. It saddens me deeply that even though they are basically good people, in their minds, life is a lost cause.

For most of us, heaven and hell are never at the forefront of what we do, but they still haunt us from behind the scenes, tugging on our feelings and attitudes, playing on our deepest fears. A few years ago, I was visiting an older lady from my congregation. She was always warm and pleasant and seemed like a generally positive person. But as sometimes happens with folks in the twilight of their years, she had become distressingly preoccupied with thoughts about death. She wasn't worried about her own death or contemplating suicide or anything like that. No, she simply found herself ruminating on the possible fates of her friends and family whom she had seen slip away over the years. As her mind worked through the gallery of names and faces of all those she had loved and lost, she kept coming back to her father. She told me about how she loved her dad more than anyone; how, of all her many siblings, she was always the apple of his eye; and how, even as he grew old, crotchety, and stubborn as a mule, she could still see him with the soft eyes of her youth.

Her father had died about twenty years prior; as the woman talked about him, she suddenly broke down into tears, almost unable to speak. In counseling situations, I always have to suppress my initial instinct to rush over to try to console those who are weeping. So I did my best to just stay put and let her work through her emotions. Finally, after a few minutes of sobbing and catching her breath, she was able to blurt out, "I hope hell isn't as bad as they say."

I was bewildered. It was an odd thing for someone to say about a person they loved so much. "What on earth makes you think your father is in hell?" I couldn't help but inquire.

"My son," she said. "He goes to church every week, very devout, studies the Bible, and he told me, 'You just can't go to heaven if you don't believe in Jesus.'"

"Didn't your father believe in Jesus?" I asked.

"Dad just didn't care," she explained, still crying. "He came to church a few times but spent most Sundays fishing or watching football. He wasn't against God per se. It just wasn't, you know, his thing. It was a nonissue."

She went on to talk at some length about how one day her son pulled out his Bible to show her all these verses that told her that her father was in hell. I still can't imagine what it must be like for your son to inform you of his grandfather's damnation at your kitchen table. A few days later, she overheard her son flippantly tell his own children that their great-grandpa was burning in torment.

Ever since then, the woman had been plagued with nightmares about her dad being tortured by devils. She confessed to me that even though she knew it probably wouldn't work, she prayed that God would ease his suffering. "I know he doesn't answer those kinda prayers," she said, "but I gotta pray 'em anyway."

I was struck by that thought. What must it be like to love someone so much that after twenty years you still pray for them every day, even though you think your prayers are falling on deaf ears? I couldn't imagine pleading with my heavenly Father, year after year, for my own earthly father, all the while believing that God was just waving away my prayers like flies. How could I sing the praises of a God who wouldn't help my dad? How could I call *that* God a God of love?

She wiped her eyes and forced a smile, as if resigning herself to this life of unanswered prayer. She quoted Isaiah 55:8: "For my thoughts are not your thoughts, nor are your ways my ways, says the Lord." And with that, her tears dried up, and she was ready to move on in the conversation; I, however, would think about that response for days. To me, it seemed like she wasn't so much quoting a Bible verse as she was using it to cast a kind of magic spell over herself, like an enchantment that allowed her to suppress all her pain, fear, and frustration under a thin veneer of "what the Bible says." In that moment, I think she was, at least on some level, aware of the contradiction she was feeling, an incongru-

ence between God's dual roles of infinitely loving Father and infinitely wrathful executioner, an incompatibility that, if ever fully
comprehended, could make her lose her faith altogether . . . but
thankfully, she had a Bible verse. For her, that quote was a pithy
aphorism that she could hold in her memory and have at her
disposal to use whenever she needed to inoculate herself against
the obvious cognitive dissonance of believing simultaneously in
a God of love and in a hell of endless conscious torment. It was
an anchor in the midst of a storm of contradiction.

That was the day I decided that, if nothing else, I needed to
acknowledge this terrible incongruity, both for my own sake and
for the sake of my ministry. I couldn't simply ignore the issue
any longer. It became clear to me that there were people in my
congregation who were, though still very much alive and, as far
as I knew, still very much within the loving embrace of their God,
nevertheless *tormented* by hell. Hell was a very clear, frightening,
and baffling presence in their lives because they feared it either for
themselves or for their friends and family. No matter how much I
preached about the unconditional acceptance and forgiveness of
God, part of them would always be captive to the ominous horror
of eternal retribution. For their sake, I had to stop waving off the
apparent incongruence. I had to resist the urge to short-circuit
the cognitive dissonance and instead seek to interrogate those
two visions of God: Divine Lover and Vengeful Punisher. It was
a calling to dive deep into the paradox of God's love and wrath,
God's grace and judgment, and see what there was to find, no
matter how uncomfortable or even doctrine-shattering it might
be. This book is the fruit of that labor.

it seemed *good*

I know the premise of this book is both provocative and challeng-
ing, but if you are someone who finds yourself provoked, I hope
you'll take the challenge.

If you are someone who has left the church of your childhood, grown weary over the constant threats of judgment and damnation that churches have used to assert their power, or are otherwise going through the profound process that has come to be known as deconstruction, I hope you will find a measure of healing in these pages. My desire is that you will find hope for the church you've considered leaving and that you'll be convinced that while Christians are often condemning, Christianity need not be.

Likewise, if you're someone from a fundamentalist, evangelical, or nondenominational background, I covet your attention the most. If you're someone who knows what you believe, someone who is supremely concerned with the values, convictions, and integrity of your faith, I pray that you might be willing to undertake that rarest of twenty-first-century American activities: to sit down and engage an opinion with which you may disagree.

These days it's all too easy to go through life hearing only the opinions that we want to hear. We have "friends" on social media we can cancel, block, or even quietly "unfriend" upon any whiff of those opinions we deem to be just too noxious to hear. We can sign up to have our inboxes loaded with news stories tailored to our personal political tastes. Is there any question that this new "age of information" has actually become the "age of the echo chamber"? Gone are the days when we would have to put up with the irritants of divergent opinions. Now we can cocoon ourselves in hermetic bubbles of technology where we can choose to listen only to those voices that parrot our own thoughts and beliefs back to us. That's why it can be almost impossible to find spaces where big ideas and diverse opinions can be calmly considered without shock and outrage, even among Christians.

Likewise, we now have "alternative facts," which is just a short way of saying, "the ones in power get to decide what the truth is." Of course, history tells us that this has always been the case, but the current state of our politics and media has placed the issue front and center. Never before in my lifetime has the idea of truth been so obviously partisan and so deeply polarizing. As I talk with friends and family and with members of my church and community, it has become clear that this polarization has created a crisis of thought in which most folks simply don't know what to believe or whom they can trust anymore. Whether we are talking about politics, racism, climate science, or—most pressingly as was the case during the COVID-19 pandemic—epidemiology, it seems as if our whole society is consumed in a battle over who gets to decide which truth gets to win. These past few years, it has felt like a *total* war, with all our young people out on the front lines and grandmas and grandpas growing "victory gardens" of resentment at home. Increasingly, when people are faced with this confusing no-man's-land of cognitive attrition, most simply pick a side and go with it. To hell with everyone else.

Unfortunately, this whole state of affairs plays directly into the hands of one of Christianity's most ignominious legacies: the constant correlation of authority and certainty. It seems that ever since her founding, the church in every age and place has secretly relied on a pernicious, unstated, but almost universal fallacy: the idea that the authority of our leaders is directly proportional to the amount of certainty they can project. The more sure they are, the more we seem to trust them. The more they can confidently and doubtlessly explain to us the exact state of the world (and the afterlife), the more likely we are to listen. The louder and more insistent they are, the more receptive we become.

As an older teenager, I was an assistant to the youth pastor at our church. He had a heart for ministry, especially for students— so much so that he made sure that just about every student he met had the opportunity to "get saved." He loved nothing more than convincing previously carefree, secular teenagers that (1) they were, in fact, sinners; (2) "the wages of sin is death" (Rom. 6:23; otherwise known as a hell of endless torment); and (3) their only hope to avoid this awful fate was to believe in Jesus and invite him into their hearts.

The youth pastor was impressively good at his job, and our youth group was always growing with kids who declared faith in Jesus for the very first time. Of course, I didn't know it at the time, but now as I look back, I can plainly see that he was able to accomplish this growth only because he managed to project an aura of absolute certainty.

Twice a year we would throw huge parties with pizza and games, and all the kids were asked to bring their friends. Then, at the end of the night, we would gather everyone together and slow everything down so the youth pastor could give a "talk," where he set about the task of convincing the crowd of teenagers that they needed to believe in Jesus in order to avoid an eternity of very physical-sounding torture. He talked about the sensation of burning and the desperation of wanting the pain to stop, yet never getting relief. He loved to use clever analogies to explain the concept of eternity. I remember something about a seagull taking one grain of sand from a beach every ten thousand years. And all of these rich descriptions were littered with words and phrases like "absolutely," "believe me," and "you can bet on it." He constantly referred to the Bible as the "Word of God," and whenever one of the kids would challenge something, he would appear astonished and say, "Look, I'm just giving you the Word of God. If you wanna argue with it, you're gonna have to take it up with him. I'm just telling you what God says."

In the three years that we worked together, I don't remember him ever once admitting any uncertainty, doubt, or ambivalence—about what the Bible means, his interpretation of it, or anything else for that matter. His mantra was always, "The Bible says it, I believe it, and that settles it."

I looked up to the man. Back then, I thought that was just how preachers were supposed to talk. But as I grew in my own calling and in my own ministry, I had to reckon with his impact on my life and my faith. When I actually studied the Bible as something other than God's exact transcription of "life's little instruction manual"; when I was confronted with stories, symbols, and poetry from civilizations and languages that no longer exist; when I began to wrestle with the history of the church, both saintly and sinful, I always had that youth pastor's voice in my head, telling me that faith was all or nothing, take it or leave it, God's Truth or no truth.

That voice was finally silenced one night in college as I pored over my notes for a class. While reading, I stumbled across the Jerusalem Council in Acts 15, and it struck me as it never had before. For context, the apostles had gathered for a council in Jerusalem to hash out whether gentile converts to the faith were required to submit to the Jewish purity codes, circumcision being chief among them. This appears to be the first real doctrinal controversy in Christianity.

When the council was over, they sent a letter to the churches stating their decision. The amazing thing about that letter is that it doesn't use the kind of language we would expect today. It doesn't declare anything as God's Holy Word. It doesn't threaten those who dissent or condemn anyone as a heretic on the opposite side. It makes no pretense of being inerrant, infallible, inarguably correct Truth. Rather, the apostles start by saying, "It seemed good to the Holy Spirit and to us . . ."

"It *seemed* good . . ." I hadn't ever heard a Christian leader talk that way before. These were the apostles after all, the guys (and back then I had wrongly assumed that they were all men) who knew what they were talking about! If anyone had the right to not mince words, to lay it all out, to tell it like it is, it was them. They were the ones who had the anointing and the authority. They should have known how important it was to be clear, adamant, and resolute in the Truth. They should have been unwavering in their commitment. They should have used words like "absolutely," "believe us," and "you can bet on it."

But they didn't take that bait. No, instead they stated their opinion in such a way as to seemingly acknowledge that they may

have been wrong, or at least that they may have misinterpreted
. . . something. By appealing to the Holy Spirit, it's almost as if
they conceded that there was something inherently ethereal and
mystical in what they were attempting to say, that the kind of
doctrinal work they were doing was an inexact science. In a subtle way, that first encyclical letter, that first real piece of written
Christian doctrine, leaves room for the leaders of the church to
admit that they may have missed something—that they may not
have gotten it right.

That day, as I studied Acts 15, the first flower of mystery blos-
somed in my soul, and it wasn't long until the whole garden was
in full bloom. I realized then that I, like much of the church of this
age, had mistaken conviction for faith.

So in the spirit of the Jerusalem Council and that first encyclical, allow me to state the thesis of the work now before you: it
seems to me that hell does not exist . . . at least not in the way that
we've been raised to think it does. Whatever hell there may be, it
is not and cannot be a place of endless torment. If it were, then
God would simply not be God, the atoning work of Jesus Christ
would be a cruel joke, and even heaven would be a torturous
prison. If hell is a place where unrepentant sinners are constantly
and perpetually tormented, then all of us would be tormented
with them. If hell is *that* hell, then we are already there.

But since I believe that God is God, that Jesus Christ did atone
for the sins of the world, and that the promise of eternal life is
sealed within us, I must argue that hell, if it exists at all, is undoubtedly something completely different and that the scope of
Christ's atoning work is universal.

Put differently, it seems to me that if anyone is saved, everyone
is saved . . . no matter what.

That's what I think, anyway. I wouldn't say that I'm *certain*
about it because, as I will also argue, the very nature of the afterlife
is beyond certainty, beyond the kind of resolute conviction that
has unfortunately become the calling card of the church today.

Rather, this book is intended to be a strike against that kind of certainty—the kind of certainty that keeps elderly women up at night worrying about the fates of their fathers and their stillborn babies, the kind that tortures those who can't seem to escape the sins of their past, and the kind that makes innocent teenagers weep as they are invited to contemplate the ridiculous, almost pornographic horrors of eternal torture. If the arguments I offer here cause even a crack in someone's certainty that hell is a place of never-ending torture, then all the hours of work will have been well worth it.

But here's what I am certain about: The hell of everlasting pain is used as a weapon. It is used to keep us afraid, confused, and submissive. It is used by those, like me, who are in positions of trust and power to hold on to their authority, to divide and subjugate the ones who trust them and depend on them to make holy mysteries tangible. In other words, hell isn't so much the vessel of the damned as it is an instrument of damnation.

And I'm absolutely *certain* that you don't believe in it.

what we talk about
when we talk about hell

It is hard to understand the psychology of pious Christians who calmly accept the fact that their neighbors, friends, and relatives will perhaps be damned. I cannot resign myself to the fact that the man with whom I am drinking tea is doomed to eternal torments.

—Russian Orthodox theologian Nikolai Berdyaev,
The Destiny of Man

When I was seven years old, my teenage cousin took me aside at a family picnic and quietly confessed to me that he no longer believed in God. I could tell that he was torn up about it, but he seemed resolute. "I just can't believe in all those silly legends and fairy tales anymore," he said, holding back his tears.

"Why did you tell me?" I asked.

"Well, because I know that you're the only one in the family who would understand, and you would never break my confidence."

I immediately broke his confidence.

And *of course* I did! As far as I was concerned, my cousin was going to hell! According to what I was raised to believe, that meant that he was going to suffer forever and ever, that he would be burning and gnashing his teeth (whatever that meant) while the rest of us were up in heaven with Jesus. I couldn't just let that go! So I wagged my finger and started screaming at him to change his mind, warning him of the eternal destruction that awaited upon his death. When he refused to repent, I had to tell someone. I ran out to the gazebo where the family was having their picnic, rushed up to my mom, buried my head in her lap, and sobbed, "He's going to burn! He's going to burn!"

another sip of tea

Now that I'm older, I wonder: where did I get all that from? I don't remember any Sunday school teachers telling me that hell was an eternity of fire. I'm certain it was never the theme of Vacation Bible School. I can't recall any felt-board characters that looked to be twisted with agony. Yet the message got across, as it often does (especially to children). When I was in that moment as a child, facing the cosmic scale and eternal proportions of heaven and hell, I did what only seemed right: I cried. I screamed. I tattled.

Have you ever had a similar experience? Have you ever worried about someone close to you going to hell? How do you even *respond* when someone reveals something like that? Do you argue with them? Maybe passively invite them to church every Sunday morning until they give in? Is it best to yell and scream? Or, like the friends of Nikolai Berdyaev, do you just take another sip of tea and keep living your life?

In the years since, especially since I've been pastoring, I've had many people tell me that they didn't believe in God anymore. Some of them were close to me. Some I hardly knew. Some were even fellow clergy. Surprisingly, I've never once gotten as upset as I did back when I was seven. Now, when someone tells me that they've lost their faith, I just try to be "pastoral" and understanding. I ask questions, I don't argue, and I certainly don't tell anyone.

But back then, when I was a child faced with the gravity of that situation, when I thought someone's eternal destiny might be at stake, all I could think to do was throw a fit.

And you know what? If hell is what they say it is, if it is the endless torture of souls after death, then seven-year-old Derek was right, and thirty-eight-year-old Derek is woefully and tragically wrong. Yelling, screaming, and throwing a hissy fit are perfectly proportional and appropriate responses to the news that someone you love is going to burn forever and ever. The idea that a loved one could face a hopeless future of such unimaginable horror should lead us to respond with as much force, emotion, and fervor as possible. Little Derek pulled out all the stops because he knew what he believed: if you don't believe in God, if you don't have Jesus in your heart, then your destiny is a hell of everlasting torment. My actions that day confirmed that belief.

So let me ask again. How would *you* respond, and what does your response say about the hell you *really* believe in?

When I infer that you don't really believe in hell, I'm not trying to be combative. I'm trying to draw a line between that which we truly believe and that which we merely *think* we believe. Christians do this all the time. That's why we quote Paul when he says, "Examine yourselves to see whether you are living in the faith" (2 Cor. 13:5), and Jesus warns us, "Not everyone who says to me, 'Lord, Lord,' will enter the kingdom of heaven" (Matt. 7:21).

After a life spent in the church, I've noticed that Christians tend to walk around with an unspoken insecurity, a nagging feeling that they may not actually believe the things they say they believe. Don't get me wrong—I think that's a good thing. We *should* be suspicious of what we actually believe. We should interrogate our beliefs. If our collective history has proved anything over the years, it's that we humans have this tremendous power to deceive even our own minds, assuring ourselves that we believe something, when, in practice, our lives betray the fact that we don't believe it at all.

When your friend spends all her time talking about climate change, and she criticizes you for not having solar panels or for eating food that isn't sourced locally, and then you see her climb into a gas-guzzling SUV, you can sniff out that there's a problem: her beliefs don't match her actions. Likewise, when a preacher gets up in front of the congregation and gives sermon after sermon about "sexual purity," and then someone finds a whole load of pornography on his hard drive, that's a problem. We call those kinds of problems "hypocrisy," and the usual way that Christians deal with them is telling the hypocrite, in no uncertain terms, that they need to bring their actions in line with their beliefs. What I'm doing here is quite the opposite. When it comes to hell, I say there's a hypocrisy between our beliefs and our lives, but I happen to think that it's actually our beliefs that need to change.

Eighty-two percent of all evangelical Christians say that they believe in a "hell of eternal judgment."[1] My argument is that if they really and truly believed that—if they were, as Paul says, living in that faith—then the stakes would be so high, the danger so imminent, the anxiety so great that we would hardly recognize them at all. If they really believed that the damned were resigned to an eternity of burning torment, they wouldn't be able to sit back and take another sip of tea. Their lives would be fundamentally different from how they are now, and their ministry of salvation would be all-consuming.

the ten-thousand-year seagull

The idea that hell is a landscape of everlasting torment has become so common, so utterly ubiquitous and ingrained into the fabric of our spiritual lives, that it can be hard to see the full implications of what such a belief would mean to our day-to-day existence. First, we need to parse what we mean when we say "eternal" and "torment" if we can ever hope to evaluate the idea objectively.

The various Christian traditions and denominations all have their own interpretations of what exactly the word "eternal" means in regard to hell. I think you would agree that, for most people, it simply means that hell is never-ending, that hell runs on an unstoppable clock and a calendar of endless pages. I will take issue with that definition of the word in chapter 7, but for now let's assume that when most people use the word "eternal," they mean "everlasting." As my youth pastor put it, "Hell is like that seagull coming every ten thousand years to pick up one grain of sand from the beach. And when the last grain is gone, it will have only just begun."

I've seen a lot of preachers, youth pastors, and evangelists get a real kick out of finding the most interesting and provocative ways of describing the eternity of hell, but it seems to me that no matter how novel their analogies may be, they never really grasp the true implication of what they are saying: that the limited span of a human life, however long it may be, is actually so short that it is *literally inconsequential* when compared to the infinite time of eternity. If the average human lived a thousand years or even a million years, we would have the same problem. Comparing any fixed number to infinity renders the number effectively zero. If we really believed that our everlasting life was solely dependent on the finite number of years we spend on earth, then every moment of every day of every year here on earth would be so precious and direly important that we wouldn't be able to live anything even approaching a "normal" life.

By comparison, let's imagine that you're on a two-week cruise to the Bahamas. On day five, while you are relaxing alone by the pool, you see a child trip over the railing and fall overboard into the passing ocean below. You are startled and upset, but, after considering your options for a moment, you realize that you may never have the money or the opportunity to go on a cruise again. You see the life preserver hanging near the spot where the child fell. After some quick mental math, you figure that it would take only about thirty seconds to throw the life preserver out to the child. You probably wouldn't mind spending thirty seconds of a once-in-a-lifetime cruise to save a young life . . . but then you realize that you would have to take the time to pull the child back into the boat. What happens if they don't grab the life preserver? Would you have to call for help? How long would that take to arrive? And of course, even under the best of circumstances, there would probably be mountains of paperwork to fill out afterward. You might have to give a statement to the captain. The parents would want to ask you what happened . . .

. . . Hmm. On second thought, you decide to stay put. After all, you're only on this trip because God must have wanted you to enjoy yourself, and while you may be sad about the child's death, you take a sip of your umbrella drink and decide that you really just need to keep living your life.

If we really and truly believed in an eternal hell, if we could actually grasp the stakes of that, then living a regular life—doing things like reading, having hobbies, or going on a trip—would be like refusing to take thirty seconds out of a two-week vacation to throw a life preserver to a drowning child. Refusing to spend even an entire lifetime trying to save souls would be a moral outrage if we compared it to the infinite calendar of eternity.

When we start to imagine that our lives exist for the sake of a cause that is infinite in scale, it quickly becomes very difficult to defend the idea of doing anything not directly related to that cause. Eating, drinking, and sleeping become acceptable only to the extent that they help further the mission. Going to the movies would be unconscionable. A quick cup of coffee would be considered a dangerous and irresponsible indulgence. The ministry of salvation would take over our every waking moment, and rightly so. There could be no greater enterprise, no more worthy purpose, than to sacrifice every second of these finite little lives for the sake of those who might spend an eternity in hell.

Our every conversation would be akin to a miniature Billy Graham crusade, and even he would be regarded as a slacker for taking days off and spending so much time with his family. We would condemn him at his funeral: "He had all eternity to enjoy a never-ending state of bliss! Why didn't he work harder while he was still here? He could have saved one more."

Wait. Strike that. If we actually believed that hell was eternal, why would we take the time to bury our dead?

the impossibility of hopelessness

In the same way, I've heard those same youth pastors, preachers, and evangelists go on about how hopeless an eternity in hell would be. Again, we throw around the word "hopeless" so casually that we haven't reckoned with what it means. For instance, in Dante Alighieri's *Inferno*, undoubtedly the most popular description of hell in all of Christian history, there is a sign hanging above the vestibule of hell that reads "All abandon hope, ye who enter here."[2] I doubt that the human mind can even grasp that idea—the absence of *all* hope. In a way, that's actually a tougher thing to imagine than eternity. We have some grasp of time, so in our minds, we can just project that idea out into the future, but we have no conception of what it is to be *truly* and *completely* hopeless.

When we use that word, it's always situational: "the battle was hopeless," "this relationship is hopeless," and so on. However, none of us, no matter how cynical we might be, have no hope inside of us whatsoever. Hope is always there, in some form or another, as a goodness that pulls us forward in life, some desire that somehow tomorrow might be a little better than today. I've had very serious depression, anxiety, and PTSD, and at no time would I say that I was anywhere close to being devoid of hope. I'd be willing to argue that even those who are suicidal don't have access to that depth of hopelessness. After all, even suicide itself, as tragic and heartbreaking as it is, is still at its core an act of hope, a desperate search for release, for an end to an intolerable pain.

Even for an atheist who doesn't believe in the afterlife at all, death and nonexistence can be preferable to a truly agonizing life. Even the idea of pure nothingness can be a light to those caught in a tunnel of suffering—but hell, as the place of eternal torment we Christians imagine it to be, would be barren of any optimism, anticipation, or promise of anything that could rightly be called "good," even the sweet release of death.

Even forgetting about the pain and the torment, just the idea that God would allow for the possibility that some of God's children might dwell forever in that kind of despair ought to scandalize us. It should make Christians question whether the God they worship is truly a God of love.

a childish hell

Of course, it isn't enough to say that hell is just a place of eternal hopelessness. No, hell just wouldn't be hell without the torment, the unstoppable, unimaginable pain visited upon the damned. Truth be told, for all the preachers I've known and all the books I've read, I've never really understood what it means to say that hell is full of this unrelenting agony. What would such pain even *be* in the afterlife?

Those who peddle the doctrine of hell are quick to point to stories in the Bible like the "rich man" who is said to be burning (Luke 16:19–31) and the "weeping and gnashing of teeth" (Luke 13:28; Matt. 13:42, 50; 22:13; 24:51; 25:30). We will get to those passages in detail later on, but for now my question is, Do damned souls have some sort of skin with nerve endings capable of feeling a burn? Do they have tear ducts with which to weep? Teeth to gnash? I suppose we have to acknowledge that these are all analogies, poetic symbols of the spiritual misery that awaits the damned.

Did you ever notice that these analogies are almost always physical? Certainly there are other kinds of pain—emotional pain, psychological pain, the pain of humiliation, the pain of grief—yet no one ever talks about those being the pains of hell. I've never seen a description of hell as the experience of losing a dying loved one over and over again, or being forced to do something terrible like torture an innocent child or beat a helpless animal. I've never heard of a hell of endless rape. Even the worst that Dante was able to come up with was getting picked over by birds, being roasted in burning tombs, and having a plague of itching, oozing scabs. None of those things sound particularly pleasant, but they are at least imaginable, like amplified versions of the pains that we humans experience every day. The only thing in the *Inferno* that borders on the truly dehumanizing is the fate of flatterers: being buried in shit.[3]

My point is that the pains of hell are usually thought to be brutal yet uncomplicated, harsh but stupid. This version of hell isn't about taking away your human dignity or self-worth, causing an existential crisis, or (especially not) making you consider the error of your ways. Neither emotion nor contrition nor reform have anything to do with this version of damnation. In this hell, pure, unadulterated agony is the point. The message seems to be, "Hell hurts! It burns! It makes you cry forever!" Come to think of it, it seems almost like a lesson that's been specifically tailored to children.

As long as we think about it like children, it seems easy to comprehend. After all, our earthly parents sometimes hurt us and make us cry, whether it's through spanking, grounding, scolding, or taking away a cell phone. Sometimes a child gets a cut, and they know the parent has to spray that stinging stuff on it in order to make it better. Sometimes a kid has to drink yucky medicine. We implicitly understand the pain that sometimes has to flow from parent to child.

The difference is that the pain that is passed from parent to child always has (or at least always should have) some good at the end of it. We get the stinging spray and the yucky medicine in order to heal and feel better. We may get spanked or sent to time out so we learn a lesson. The pain has an end, a telos, a goal. There's a love behind it that even as children we come to understand.

The threat of everlasting pain, however, has no telos. It has no goal, no ultimate good on the other side. If it never ends, then it can never bring about anything good or loving at all. It's just punishment for the sake of punishment—pain for the sake of pain.

Some will argue that the torment of hell somehow serves the glory of God, and others may say that the damned choose it for themselves, that the true source of their pain is not God but rather their own free will. We will get back to those ideas later on, but for now it's enough to ask the question, At what point does refusing to stop someone's pain actually become torture?

Certainly, we have to allow some people to feel pain sometimes. That's why we don't give morphine to every kid who scrapes her knee (at least not anymore), but that's not the kind of pain we are talking about. By definition, an everlasting hell neither heals nor teaches. That's actually the express purpose of this version of hell: that no reform is possible, that the debt can never be repaid. The pain of hell is specifically *unredemptive*. Rather, the pain exists for its own sake; its only intended purpose is to be felt by the one who is suffering forever and ever.

I'll put it another way. If God created the place where the pain happens, if God created the mechanism by which the pain happens, if God knows the pain is happening, and if the all-powerful God can stop it from happening yet refuses to intervene, then God must *mean* for it to happen. God wills the pain. Even if it's the result of someone's own free will, even if it is (somehow) just, even if God isn't actively causing it by poking them with pitchforks or lighting the matches under their toes, by simply having the power to stop it and then choosing not to, God is responsible for the pain.

Let's be clear: to believe in a hell of endless torment is to believe that God tortures.

Allow me to draw an analogy of my own.

Let's say my wife and I are out on a walk one night, and a vicious dog comes running out of the bushes and brutally mauls my wife. I fight back to the extent that I'm able, but she is hurt badly, and she dies of her wounds in the hospital. I am, of course, utterly distraught. No greater tragedy could possibly befall my life than to lose my wife. Taking her from me is literally the greatest crime any person or beast could commit against me. And it's especially tragic given that my wife was a dog lover. Me too.

As I grieve in her hospital room, a police officer comes to take my statement. Halfway through, he gets a call, then turns to me and says, "I know it will be of little consolation to you, but we found the dog, and we are going to have it destroyed." Surprisingly, I ask him not to do that, but instead to have the dog released into my custody. The officer is confused, but he begrudgingly agrees, thinking that I must want to somehow rehabilitate the creature. In fact, nothing could be further from the truth.

On the way home, I stop at the office of a friend who happens to be a veterinarian. There, I procure several units of dog blood in IV bags, a canine feeding tube, a saline drip, and some kind of paralytic drug that will render the dog immobile yet fully conscious. When I get home, I take the dog, the medical supplies, and a tool box down to my basement. My plan is to lay the dog out on my table, chemically immobilize it, and torture it for as long as I can possibly keep it alive. No matter how much it howls or whimpers, I won't stop until it dies. The torture would go on for hours, certainly, but with the feeding tube, saline, and extra blood, I might be able to draw it out for days or even weeks, if I'm careful.

Before I go further, let me say that this scenario was as painful for me to write as it was for you to read. I include it only because I want to make it clear that this is the kind of torture we are talking about when we talk about a hell where God tortures human beings for all eternity.

The point of that story is that what I do to the dog is actually less horrific than what we imagine that God does to damned souls in hell! I could at least understand how the grief of losing a loved one might potentially drive an already-unbalanced individual to do something so hateful to an animal or even another person. We have hormonal and psychological bonds to our spouses and families and friends that are, in some circumstances, capable of creating that kind of emotion. It's possible to have some sort of severe mental illness that makes a response like murder and torture seem justified in the moment. Given the right confluence of factors, gory violence can seem like the most appropriate response to a frail and hurting human mind. The difference, however, is that God isn't hurt by what we do, at least not in the same way that humans can be hurt. God's mind isn't subject to the same frailties as our own. If God is all those things the philosophers have always said—omnipotent, omniscient, invincible, and unchanging—then God cannot be *harmed* the same way we can. Put simply, we can't hurt God because we are too small and God is too big.

It's like a frustrated four-year-old running up to his mom and punching her legs as hard as possible. The mom doesn't punch back and the police don't charge the child with assault because the child can't hurt the mom. There's no crime I could commit, from idolatry to genocide, that could be anything more than a weak punch in God's almighty thigh.

Likewise, even if we could hurt God, there's a point at which punishment for any crime becomes gratuitous. That's why some states explicitly allow some criminals to be put to death for some particularly heinous crimes, but no state (at least in principle) allows for a criminal to be tortured for any crime. This is because torture is inherently revolting to most human beings (though obviously, not all). The vast majority of the human race simply has too much inborn empathy. We become more scandalized by the pain we inflict than we are by the initial crime itself. There is a threshold at which guilt collapses into vulnerability. The crime is hidden underneath the whines and the whimpers of the criminal. No matter how heinous the offense or how objectionable the offender, there is always a point of pain that elicits pity for the victim.

So then the argument must be that, somehow, God is *less* empathetic than we are? That the God of love somehow brackets that love—for all eternity, mind you—in order to torture God's own children? How long can God withhold God's love for even one individual and still be considered a God of love?

the hell you don't believe in

The use of crude veterinary techniques to keep the dog alive for as long as possible is another weak comparison to the vile idea that God keeps souls alive to be tortured in hell. And yes, that is my argument: if hell is eternal torment, then God is actively keeping those souls alive.

Most of those who profess a belief in this kind of hell assume that our lives, whether on this side of death or the other, are somehow self-sustaining—that like the Energizer Bunny, our souls just keep going and going, all by themselves. This denies a fundamental teaching of Christianity: that our existence, both in this world and the next, is fully dependent upon God. Theologians have had different ways of saying this, that God is "the well of existence," "the ground of being," or "the source of ontology." They all mean roughly the same thing: we exist only because God wills it so, or as Paul quoted, "For 'In him we live and move and have our being'" (Acts 17:28). Christianity has always spoken with a single voice on this. We only continue to "be" every moment because God continues to infuse us with being. If God ever stopped granting life to our souls, then we wouldn't just die. We would literally fall out of existence.

This is why it's so odd to hear Christians casually refer to hell simply as "separation from God" and attribute the pain of hell to nothing more than the natural consequence of being disconnected from our Creator. We can't be "separated" from God, because all existence, as Paul said, is in God. To be fully separated from God would be the same as being separated from the source of our existence. To be cut off from God would be not to exist at all.

So if souls are alive to experience an eternity of conscious torment, then God is actively and purposely keeping them alive. If no rehabilitation is possible, then God is keeping the IV drip of existence flowing into their souls for no other reason than that they may continue to endure an utterly pointless eternal pain. We have a name for that sort of thing. It's called sadism. At some point, we have to call a hell of eternal torment what it is: blasphemy against the character of God.

But, thankfully, none of us *really* believe in a hell of eternal torment. If we really did, then we would all be seven-year-old Dereks. We would scream and wail in the faces of atheists every day and work ourselves to the bone trying to convert those of other religions. If we really thought that every moment of the day people were dying and their souls were falling into some bottomless lake of fire where they would endure nonstop torture, if we really believed that, then "public evangelist" would be the only acceptable full-time job. We would be out there beating the pavement, rain or shine, preaching our guts out, screaming the gospel of Jesus Christ at every passerby we could find. A sandwich board bearing a warning about the wrath to come would be the universal Christian uniform. We would all be living on the streets, eating garbage, and sleeping wherever we could and only whenever we had to just to keep the ministry of evangelism going as much as possible.

Every person we met would be sitting on the precipice of the worst fate imaginable, just one brain aneurysm or heart attack away from an infinity of pain! If death is the (seemingly arbitrary) cutoff point for developing a saving faith in Jesus Christ, then every living person would constitute an emergency. No cushy job inside an air-conditioned office. No ball games on Saturday afternoon. No time for sex. Those things are only distractions.

Each of us has but maybe ninety short years on this planet. If that kind of hell exists, then not to use every moment of every day to save souls would be morally repugnant.

Back in seminary, a group of us were discussing the differences between evangelicals and mainline Protestants, and someone brought up the traditional mainline emphasis on social justice. One of the more conservative evangelical students boiled over with frustration and blurted out, "Why should we *waste our time* to feed and clothe the damned?" We were all silent, stunned by the callousness of her statement. But, as I think about it ten years later, I realize that she had a point. In a world where we imagine that souls are being lost every day to never-ending torture, doing things like feeding the hungry and clothing the naked would be a pointless distraction.

If you're thinking to yourself, "I've never thought about it that way before," allow me to suggest that, if you really believed in that kind of hell, you would have. If the concept of eternal conscious torment was truly present to your mind as an actual possibility, you wouldn't be able to help but think about it that way. Your life, as you currently live it, would be utterly transformed. You would never drive a car, lest you get in an accident and kill someone who had yet to hear the gospel. You'd stand at the entrance to the hospital shouting about Jesus and salvation. You would never accept a friend or a family member who rejected the Christian faith. All the violent means of conversion from the Middle Ages and the Spanish Inquisition would start to make much more sense. The foul tactics of Westboro Baptist Church would seem reasonable and appropriate.

Likewise, you would never procreate. If you truly thought there was even a possibility that your children might end up in a hell of endless torture, you would never take that chance. Even those who were committed to raising their children in the Christian faith, having them baptized as soon as they were born, spending time in prayer and Bible study every night before bed

... none of it would ever be enough to assuage your constant worry that they might backslide, that something could happen, and they could lose their faith and fall into the pit. Men would castrate themselves. Women would have their tubes tied. Procreation would be anathema.

When we talk about hell, we are talking about a place that God created and sanctioned, where God continues to keep human souls alive in a state of perpetual hopelessness in order to torture them for literally no reason. If you truly believed that you were facing such divine madness, then you would devote all your time, energy, motivation, and creativity to the never-ending struggle to save as many as you could from this arbitrary, sadistic God who demands either your obedient love or your perpetual suffering. To do anything less would be morally reprehensible.

Yet here you are, sitting comfortably, probably sipping your coffee, and taking some of that precious time to read a book, you disgusting piece of sh ...

... Just kidding.

Of course you're reading a book! And in a little while, you'll cook a nice meal, go for a walk, maybe have a talk with someone special, and head to bed after watching too much TV. Tomorrow you'll go to work, and look at art, and plant a garden, and laugh at your dog, and do all kinds of wondrous, beautiful, and terribly mundane things, and do you know why? Because somewhere deep inside you, there's a little voice, a voice that's so still and so small you don't even notice it anymore, a voice that has always been and will always be there, saying, "Everything is going to be okay." The rest of this book, with its theology, history, and biblical interpretation, is merely meant to help you listen to it.

three

a hell by any other name

Whenever we pick up the Bible, read it, put it down and say, "That's just what I thought," we are probably in trouble.

—Ellen F. Davis, *The Art of Reading Scripture*

You keep using that word . . . I do not think it means what you think it means.

—Inigo Montoya, *The Princess Bride*

Allow me to let you in on a little secret: Hell is not in the Bible. Yes, you read that right. Hell is never mentioned a single time from Genesis to Revelation. Not even once. Neither is eternal torture, never-ending hopelessness, or even "complete separation from God," whatever that means.

I know it doesn't seem that way. Of course hell is in the Bible . . . right? It's all over the place. If you asked your local fire-and-brimstone preacher, he would undoubtedly pull out his King James Bible and show you all fifty-four times that the word *hell* really does appear on those pages (they will probably be highlighted).[1] He will jump back and forth from verse to verse, skipping over hundreds of pages at a time, pointing to the "h-word" again and again while explaining just how dangerous it is to underestimate the damnation waiting for those who do not know Jesus, how it may lead you astray and perhaps contribute to the doom of your own soul. He will, in other words, try to convert you—because, even though he may not say it, he believes that if you question eternal torment, you are as good as lost already.

Very few things will ignite the passion of fundamentalist preachers more than questioning the existence of hell.

But what I want you to keep in mind is that whenever you see the word *hell* printed in a Bible or you hear it preached from a pulpit or brought up in the midst of a conversation, it is always a translation—and a bad one. Even that may be too generous. *Hell* isn't even a translation so much as it is a lazy English substitution, not just for one word, but for several different words and ideas.

Over the centuries this poor translation work has permeated our Christian culture and stained almost every translation of the Bible. It has infused and shaped our theological imaginations to the point that we cannot envision a God of infinite love without somehow also imagining a hell of eternal torment. Some of us can't even read the Scriptures devotionally without seeing the specter of damnation on every page, coloring every text . . . the ominous threat lurking behind every promise.

When these words and ideas are read within their own context, with attention given to the original languages and cultures that produced them, it becomes clear that they have nothing at all to do with eternal torment. But when these Scriptures are read quickly and simplistically, when they are fused together and dusted with a little morbid imagination, they form the vivid and nightmarish doctrine that Christians somehow came to enshrine as an essential (if unstated) dogma.

It will take some hard work to disentangle this web of damnation.

a snowball's chance in niflhel

On its own, *hell* is a Proto-Germanic word that comes down to us from the Norse mythology of the early Middle Ages. It originated with the Viking goddess of death, Hel, and the realm over which she held sway, Niflhel.[2] The truly odd thing about the Christian appropriation of the word is that Niflhel was never associated with any kind of fiery torture. Rather, it was understood to be a cold, misty place where nothing much ever happened.

Viking warriors who died in battle were invited to spend their afterlives feasting in the heavenly banquet halls of Valhalla, while the souls of those who died "ignoble deaths" of sickness and disease went deep into the cold earth to dwell in Niflhel. The two places weren't quite opposites, as we tend to think of heaven and hell today, so much as they were options: one was simply a reward for the honor and glory of battle, while the other was a catchall for the normal civilians.[3] Valhalla was like the first-class club of an afterlife airline while Niflhel was the fancy name they gave to the economy seats. Much like flying coach today, there wasn't anything particularly torturous about Niflhel except that it was cramped and *seemed* to go on forever.

I say "seemed" because Niflhel wasn't eternal, at least not in the sense that we think of hell as being eternal. Norse mythology understood time to be cyclical in nature, with each age of existence lasting from one Ragnarok (the Norse version of the apocalypse) to the next, gods and humans alike being reborn cycle after cycle. So Niflhel was more like a holding tank than a hell: a not-so-great beyond, a boring and chilly realm of the waiting dead. This version of the underworld had no tormenting fire, no infinity of seagulls, and not a single cry of agony. Rather Niflhel was much like an extension of medieval Nordic life: cold, misty, and mundane.

The name of hell may have come into English from the Vikings, but that doesn't mean that it's merely a translation. Rather,

I argue that because we can so easily separate it from its origins, the word *hell* has become the flavorless pill that helps us swallow the poison of eternal torment. It's become a blank slate upon which we have written an eternity of torture. Instead of grappling with the complexity of ancient and mysterious ideas, we have used the word to reduce the afterlife to a simple and horrifying choice: a heaven of bliss or a hell of pain. This biblical and theological malpractice has scarred millions of lives, turned many away from the faith, and—in the eyes of the world—maintained the church's legacy of judgment and condemnation.

the pit of sheol

In the Bible, the first word often mistranslated as *hell* is the Hebrew term *Sheol*. Of all the words mistranslated as *hell*, this is the one that bears the closest resemblance to Niflhel. It refers to a kind of gloomy and mysterious postdeath existence, and the Bible offers few clues about what it was actually like. Sheol was not even an afterlife as we might conceive of it today. It wasn't a place where fully conscious souls spent an eternity in either eternal bliss or neverending torment. Instead, it was a realm of darkness where the shadowy ghosts of the dead dwelled in a kind of nebulous existence between life and death (see Ps. 88:10; Prov. 9:18; Isa. 14:9).

The odd thing about *Sheol* is that our English translations of it tend to differ wildly. Some modern English translators have left the term untranslated, which is probably the most responsible approach. However, older translations usually translate *Sheol*, and they tend to lack any obvious consistency in the way they render the word. For instance, out of the sixty-five times that *Sheol* appears in the Hebrew Scriptures, it is translated as *hell* by the King James Version thirty-three times. The other thirty-two instances are translated as either *grave* or *pit*. But why the inconsistency?

If you look closely, a pattern begins to emerge: *Sheol* is translated as *hell* only when the context surrounding the word happens to mention punishment or bears a resemblance to eternal fiery torment. When the context seems inconsistent with that idea, it's usually translated otherwise. Throughout the ages, biblical translators have essentially cherry-picked those places where they want to apply the term *hell* in order to build their case that such a place actually exists. Put simply, if *Sheol* sounds bad, they translate it as *hell*. If it sounds neutral or even pleasant, then it becomes *grave* or *pit*.

For instance, take the story of Saul and the ghost of Samuel. The Hebrew people were explicitly forbidden to try to communicate with the disembodied ghosts of the dead (Deut. 18:9–13), yet Saul was able to enlist the help of the witch from Endor to summon the spirit of the prophet Samuel (1 Sam. 28:13–14). Upon being summoned from the darkness of Sheol, Samuel immediately complains about being disturbed (1 Sam. 28:15).

Allow me to suggest that if Samuel were, in fact, being tormented, then he might have been more appreciative to have a little break and catch his breath. Maybe he would have tried to extend the conversation a bit. Perhaps he would have asked Saul how his family was doing or about the latest news from Israel or something like that. No, at least in this passage, we get the sense that Sheol is a place of rest and that the ghosts who reside there ought not to be disturbed because they are in a state of pleasant repose, just as we write on the signs above our graves Rest in Peace. That's why here, *Sheol* is typically translated as *grave*.

Likewise, when Job is in the throes of despondency, he prays, "O that you would hide me in Sheol, that you would conceal me until your wrath is past" (Job 14:13). Can you imagine a contemporary Christian being so distraught that they would ask God to hide them in hell? That would be inconsistent with the idea of hell as we've been raised to understand it. Hell is the exact locus of God's wrath, not a place where one might take shelter from it. Perhaps that's why here the King James Version uses the term *grave*. If it were translated as *hell* then the pious reader might just question what hell is really like.

If the translators of the King James Version wanted a good passage where they could translate *Sheol* as *hell*, Deuteronomy 32:22 is a much safer bet: "For a fire is kindled in mine anger, and shall burn unto the lowest hell [Sheol], and shall consume the earth with her increase, and set on fire the foundations of the mountains." While this passage obviously has nothing to do with souls burning in eternal torment, it does mention fire and anger. For biblical translators, that's enough context to make it an acceptable use of *hell*.

Sheol also becomes *hell* when the psalmist calls down God's wrath on their enemies in Psalm 55:15 (KJV): "Let death seize upon them, and let them go down quick into hell [Sheol]: for wickedness is in their dwellings, and among them." Do you see the pattern? When the Bible speaks of the destiny of the wicked, it becomes perfectly appropriate to invoke the term that English speakers associate with eternal torment. This is justice being served: evildoers getting their divine comeuppance. When the context speaks of fire or brimstone or judgment, it's as if the translator thinks, "I'll go ahead, throw a *hell* in there." But when *Sheol* is used in any verse that would be somehow incompatible with that vision, they have to choose another word. Some other translation must be applied so as to protect the doctrine of eternal punishment from what might seem like a biblical inconsistency.

More puzzling is that the King James Version actually does render *Sheol* as *hell* in Psalm 139: "Whither shall I go from thy spirit? or whither shall I flee from thy presence? If I ascend up into heaven, thou art there; if I make my bed in hell [Sheol], behold, thou art there" (Ps. 139:7–8 KJV). At first blush it seems like Sheol is being contrasted with heaven, setting up the kind of dual afterlife that we imagine today. Hell is the bad place, heaven the good. But while it may appear as if the psalmist is being hunted by God and searching desperately for an escape from judgment, when you read the whole psalm in context you see that the author is actually praising God for having a continual presence in their life, that no matter where they are or how far they wander, God is always there, keeping them safe (v. 8), leading them by the hand (v. 10), and bringing light to their darkness (vv. 11–12).

Far from the idea that hell is a place that is somehow outside the presence of God, the psalm testifies to the idea that God's presence fills the entire creation on both sides of the grave. Even if the use of the word *hell* here were appropriate (it is not), the point would still be that God is there, still blessing, still turning darkness into light. The psalm isn't about the inescapable judgment of God. It's about the inescapable blessing and presence of God, no matter which word one chooses to use to translate *Sheol*.

I don't know about you, but that doesn't sound like the hell I learned about when I was a kid. The Hebrew Sheol can't be the hell we've been taught to fear because there aren't any instances of those who are there being in any kind of pain or torment. No matter how hard a translator might try, they can't turn Sheol into Dante's *Inferno*.

In fact, I would argue that to the Hebrew minds that wrote the Bible, Sheol wasn't an actual place at all. It wasn't a point on a map of the afterlife. It was a poetic term that was meant to convey all the mystery and ambiguity of death, the separation and alienation that happens between the living and the dead. To those who struggle, Sheol can seem like an inviting hiding place, a rock cleft for comfort and rest. To those who have just lost someone special, it feels like a bottomless pit. To those who have a guilty conscience, it feels like a coming judgment. The word itself speaks to the puzzling experience that those who have died sometime seem so very far away, and yet sometimes they seem as close as Samuel appearing like a shadow from the grave. In other words, *Sheol* is poetry. It speaks to all the ways that human beings struggle in the face of death.

Too often we try to read our two thousand years of theology back into the biblical authors instead of letting the biblical authors speak to us. We assume that they must have thought as we think, that they would desire clarity and simplicity in all things, as if standing behind the stories, poetry, and prophets of the Hebrew Scriptures there were a precise theological system, some long-lost geographical textbook of the afterlife that we can then piece together from their notes. But what we have to remember is that our spiritual ideas and theological systems have been *developed* over time. They came from different authors in different places responding to different needs. They didn't emerge as complete systems inside a hermetically sealed Bible. I would like to suggest that if the biblical authors wanted to present a systematic treatise on the nature of the afterlife, they would have done so. Instead they gave us stories and poetry, shadowy images and prophetic dreamscapes, some of which look vaguely similar to one another, and some of which look very different.

Perhaps that's why we need to own the idea that our theological tradition is ever-changing. It is a sometimes flawed and always incomplete contemporary adaptation of ancient scriptures. These texts are at times purposefully vague, mysterious, and even contradictory. The theology that you and I take for granted is a constantly shifting, still-wet mosaic assembled from fragments and broken pieces of the past, continually rearranged (within some doctrinal boundaries) to meet the challenges of the present. Some may find that description offensive or even heretical. But I happen to think it's what makes theology beautiful.

For instance, it surprises some to learn that the ancient Israelites didn't have anything even approaching a detailed understanding of the afterlife or any serious belief in the resurrection of the dead until parts of the book of Daniel were written sometime between 167 and 164 BCE (Dan. 12:1–3). There are, however, two odd stories from the book of Genesis that reveal early Israel's hazy thoughts about the afterlife that have nothing to do with heaven or hell. The first is when Abraham asks his servant to put his hand under Abraham's thigh and swear that he won't choose a daughter for Isaac from among the Canaanites (Gen. 24:1–9). The other is a similar scene in which Jacob asks his son Joseph to do the same odd ritual and swear an oath that he won't allow Jacob to be buried in Egypt, but that he will carry Jacob's body to the Promised Land (Gen. 47:29–31).

I've heard some creative preachers talk about how placing one's hand under another's thigh was some sort of sign of submission and obedience, but that's just another way contemporary Christian leaders try to cover over a mysterious scripture with something a bit more palatable to our modern minds. In actuality, Abraham and Jacob asked these men to swear their oaths while they held one another's testicles. In so doing they were swearing an oath on one another's progeny, their future, their life beyond the grave. This, the promise of children and living on through one's descendants, was the ancient Hebrew version of the afterlife—not Sheol.

Rather, Sheol was the ancient and enigmatic answer to deep questions that we modern Christians are all too quick to answer: Where are the dead? Are they still conscious? Can I speak to them? What will happen to me when I die? The biblical text offers no easy answers, but it does offer plenty of mysteries. Sheol ought to call us to humility, sobriety, and wonder rather than the certainty and arrogance of simply assuming it's just a different name for the dogmatic hell we've been raised to fear.

fetch with a three-headed dog

The New Testament is even more complex. The terms *Hades* and *Tartarus* are both often translated as *hell*. I suppose that would be simple enough, except for the fact that both of these terms come squarely from pagan Greek mythology.

If you need a bit of a refresher, Hades is the name of the Greek god of death and the realm where he reigns. Hades was one of the Olympic gods; along with his brothers Zeus and Poseidon, he successfully toppled the Titans and threw them into a pit called

Tartarus. As the spoils of their war, Zeus took over Mount Olympus, Poseidon the sea, and Hades the underworld.

If you think back to the Greek mythology you learned in elementary school, you might remember that in order to get to the underworld, the souls of the dead made their way across the River Styx and through the gate that was guarded by Cerberus, the three-headed dog. Once they passed through the gate, however, it wasn't as if they descended into some kind of volcanic cave full of fire and sulfur. No, Hades was a vast and diverse realm, an entire world unto itself.

The souls there might dwell in any one of several expansive and interesting places. Among them were the Asphodel Meadows, a huge field where those who never really amounted to anything lived in a quiet, vague sort of pasture with nothing but grass and white flowers. The grief-stricken and those who could never get past a long-lost love went to a place called the Mourning Fields. The truly righteous were sent to the Lake of Elysium and the Isle of the Blessed, where the heroes of Greek mythology, the demigods, and the morally upright would spend the afterlife in a state of perpetual bliss. In fact, the name *Elysium* literally means "to be moved with joy."

And underneath it all was a realm known as Tartarus, the underworld of the underworld, the prison of the dethroned Titans and the dungeon of the wicked. Here is the only place in all of Hades where we see actual punishment and suffering visited upon the wicked.

Prometheus was bound in chains so his liver could be eaten by a raven only for it to grow back and be consumed all over again. Sisyphus was assigned the eternal task of pushing a boulder up a hill, only to have it roll back down whenever he neared the top. The forty-nine Danaides were found guilty of murdering their husbands on their wedding night and were condemned to lug jugs of water to fill a wash basin so that they could cleanse their sins away—except that the basin was leaky and the task therefore never-ending.

You can see that Hades is not merely about eternal damnation. That may be part of it, but Hades is also about joy and peace and unrequited love and even fields of white flowers! It's not the monotone, volcanic nightmare-scape that we think of when someone says "hell." It's a vast realm of poetic irony, mystical beasts, and, yes, in one location, even something approaching torture. But if we're being honest we have to admit that even that torture isn't the same kind of blunt, stupid torture of the Christian hell. Rather, the truly painful thing about Tartarus is more like relentless monotony, an intense and frustrating kind of boredom, which isn't at all like the kind of hell we dread. The pain of those in Tartarus is more poignant than it is searing, almost like it was meant to teach a lesson, whereas for Christians, hell is simply a severe warning.

In truth, Tartarus itself is only mentioned once in the whole of the New Testament . . . sort of. In 2 Peter we read, "For if God did not spare the angels when they sinned but *cast them into hell* and committed them to chains of deepest darkness to be kept until the judgment . . ." (2 Pet. 2:4–9; emphasis mine).

The phrase "cast them into hell" is only one word in Greek, and it's weird. This passage takes a noun, the name *Tartarus*, and turns it into a verb—an action: *tartarosas*. Using it in this way undoubtedly refers to the myth of Zeus. As the story goes, upon dethroning the Titans, Zeus threw (or *cast*) the gods down into Tartarus. Essentially, 2 Peter draws a comparison between what Zeus did to the Titans and what God did to the fallen angels. If we were to mimic this use of *Tartarus* in English we might say that God "tartarized" them.

This single reference cannot be taken as a biblical confirmation of Tartarus as a real place. This passage isn't trying to say that there's an actual realm of eternal punishment any more than it would be trying to say that Zeus is a real god. *Tartarosas* describes an action, a casting down from heaven, and its use invokes a common Greek myth (with which the original audience would have been familiar) as an analogy.

Even if I were to concede that *hell* is the right term to use here (I don't), the hell in question would not be the same hell that most Christians believe in today, nor would it be the Sheol of the Hebrew Scriptures. We can definitively say that the one passage where Tartarus is mentioned is not, in fact, a reference to the eternal torment of human beings.

Unlike Tartarus, which is mentioned only once, Hades comes up several times throughout the New Testament, mostly mentioned by Jesus himself. The most famous is probably the story of the rich man and Lazarus (Luke 16:19–31), in which, as you will remember, a rich man is merciless toward a beggar in life. Once they both die, the rich man can somehow see Lazarus far off, "in the bosom of Abraham," and he begs for Abraham to tell Lazarus to come down and cool his tongue and, barring that, that Lazarus be sent to warn his brothers so that they may not come to this "place of torment" (Luke 16:28).

In sermons and Bible studies with my church, this passage always leads to discussions about heaven and hell. It elicits so many questions: Where is "the bosom of Abraham"? Why can Abraham and Lazarus see the rich man? What is it that separates them? Why is the rich man burning?

But whenever we study the passage, I always have to remind my congregation that these kinds of questions, while worthwhile, miss the point: the story of the rich man and Lazarus is one that tragically illustrates the evil of our indifference to the poor. Lazarus is a pathetic man, yearning for food, covered in sores that the dogs come and lick, yet the rich man does nothing. The rich man goes about his life with complete disregard for the poor man sitting at his gate, and then after he's dead, he has the gall to expect Lazarus to do his bidding!

The rich man is the very picture of callous opulence, and the parable illustrates how God feels about such callousness. It's a morality tale. It's the ancient Near Eastern version of a fable. There's nothing about the story that should make us think that either Lazarus or the rich man were actual people, that this conversation actually happened at some point, or that Hades (as it is thinly described here) is any kind of a definite place, the existence of which Jesus meant to endorse. Are we to assume that somewhere near the rich man we might find Cerberus playing fetch with the god Hades himself? Or that perhaps he's met the likes of Sisyphus or Prometheus?

That's just not how parables work. The story of the rich man and Lazarus is no more about hell than the parable of the sower is about farming. There was no real-life prodigal son who squandered his father's fortune. There was never any lost sheep or Good Samaritan who stopped and helped a Jew fallen by the roadside. These stories are not ripped from the headlines. That isn't their genre. Parables are universal in nature, more about life in the here and now than describing something that actually happened. They use tropes, legends, myths, and fantastical (even nonsensical) narratives to compare how we live with how we should be living.

Some Christians think that they are honoring the Bible by reading it in the most literal, straightforward way possible, as if they were reading the morning news, but that kind of interpretation (or lack thereof) disrespects the text. It turns the Holy Bible into something it was never intended to be: a genreless, simplistic tome that is somehow a spiritual analog of a contemporary textbook or instruction manual.

What's worse is that we are uncomfortable interacting with each biblical text on its own, respecting each author's individual ideas and message. Instead, we have this perceived need to conflate what every book of the Bible says with every other book, as if there is some single, undergirding theological framework that all the biblical authors are using as a reference—as if each author is referring to some shared college-level textbook of systematic theology that has since been lost to time.

I prefer an interpretation that respects the Bible for what it actually is: a multigenerational, multilingual, and multicultural work full of robust and poetic imagery, ancient sensibilities, and mysterious symbolism, all meant to elicit our wonder, curiosity, and devotion.

The story of the rich man and Lazarus is an allegory about wealth and poverty set against the common Greek myth of Hades, with which Luke's gentile audience would have been very familiar. That's also probably why he uses *Hades* again when he quotes Psalm 16, which says, "For you do not give me up to Sheol or let your faithful one see the Pit" (Ps. 16:10; quoted in Acts 2:27). The power behind the story lies in the irony of the rich man suffering in the afterlife as the poor man suffered on earth. Allow me to suggest here for the first time: I don't doubt that some will suffer in the afterlife. I don't doubt that there will be some kind of pain. But there is nothing in this passage (nor in the rest of the Bible as a whole) that declares such suffering to be eternal.

Even if there were, we would still have to ask, What happens when both Death and Hades are destroyed in the lake of fire (Rev. 20:14)?

jogging through hell

At this point in the book, I should probably mention that I've been to hell. It's really quite nice. Greener than you might expect. Lots of joggers, bicyclists, and people walking their dogs.

You see, the one word in the New Testament that is almost always translated as *hell* is the word *Gehenna*, and the thing that preachers so seldom tell their congregations is that Gehenna is an actual place . . . that can be found on a map . . . in Israel . . . and you can go there. There's even a nice park.

Long before any concept of a hell of eternal torment ever came to dawn on the mind of a theologian, there was only Gehenna, or the Valley of Hinnom, lying just southwest of the city of Jerusalem. The Valley of Hinnom was an infamous place, known throughout the generations as a cursed plot of land. The curse came as a result of the Canaanites sacrificing their children to the god Moloch there, and then the Israelite king Ahaz tried to win the favor of the gods of Damascus by sacrificing his own sons in the same spot (2 Chron. 28:23).

Recall that ever since the angel of the Lord stopped the hand of Abraham from striking down his son Isaac, the thing that set Israel apart from its neighbors, perhaps more than anything else, was that Israel's God did not condone child sacrifice. So the place where one of Israel's kings did the unthinkable became a place of infamy and dishonor.

When we have a place we want to honor, we often build a monument. What's the opposite of that? A place set aside for ignominy and degradation. That's what the Valley of Hinnom was prophesied to become: a dark heap of bodies constantly fed by the corpses of those who had no place to be buried.

The valley has long since been covered over by two thousand years of civilization that makes it an unremarkable, even pleasant place, but when the prophet Jeremiah looked out at it, he saw something very different on the horizon for Gehenna:

> Therefore the days are surely coming, says the Lord, when it will no more be called Topheth or the valley of the son of Hinnom but the valley of Slaughter, for they will bury in Topheth until there is no more room. The corpses of this people will be food for the birds of the air and for the animals of the earth, and no one will frighten them away. And I will bring to an end the sound of mirth and gladness, the voice of the bride and bridegroom in the cities of Judah and in the streets of Jerusalem, for the land shall become a waste. (Jer. 7:32–34)

It doesn't take much to see in Jeremiah's prophecy all the markings of a truly dark place just outside of Jerusalem, a wasteland where all joy and laughter has long since turned to mourning;

where birds and dogs congregate to fight over bones and scraps of flesh; and where worms and maggots would be constant and ubiquitous. This identity of Gehenna as a cursed place of rot and desolation would be made all the more stark by its proximity to the heights of the Temple Mount. Within eyeshot of one another were the mountain where all the holiness of God was pleased to dwell and, right beside it, a cursed valley that served as a reminder of the ultimate depravity of humanity. With that in mind, let's take a look at what Jesus had to say about it:

> "As for this worthless slave, throw him into the *outer darkness*, where there will be *weeping and gnashing of teeth*." (Matt. 25:30; emphasis mine)

> "If your hand causes you to sin, cut it off; it is better for you to enter life maimed than to have two hands and to go to hell [Gehenna], to the unquenchable fire. And if your foot causes you to sin, cut it off; it is better for you to enter life lame than to have two feet and to be thrown into hell [Gehenna]. And if your eye causes you to sin, tear it out; it is better for you to enter the kingdom of God with one eye than to have two eyes and to be thrown into hell [Gehenna], where their *worm never dies, and the fire is never quenched.*" (Mark 9:43–48; emphasis mine)

Do you see the connection? The outer darkness isn't some metaphysical plane outside of our own realm of existence. It's a disgusting heap of bodies just outside the walls of Jerusalem. The weeping and the gnashing of teeth aren't the reflexes of damned souls writhing in agony. They are the tears of mournful loved ones and the snarls of wild dogs. The unquenchable fire and the undying worm are turns of phrase that describe an actual geographical location, where the constant flow of bodies made the infestation of maggots unavoidable.

Jesus uses the term *Gehenna* for much the same reason that Luke and Peter used *Hades* and *Tartarus*: familiarity. Hades and Tartarus were commonplace myths and stories to which gentile listeners could relate. Gehenna was a familiar place to which the Jewish followers of Jesus could relate. If we were to do the same today, we might say something like, "They shall be thrown into Chernobyl, where the cancer always grows and the radiation never dies," or, for fans of *The Lord of the Rings*, we could refer to the "unquenchable fires of Mordor and Mount Doom."

I don't doubt that Jesus was talking about some kind of judgment, that he used the word to describe the harsh and inevitable consequences of sin and corruption. When he speaks of Gehenna, he speaks of a curse, of piles of mangled bodies mixed with garbage being consumed by worms and fire, of weeping spouses and noxious smoke. He uses those symbols for a reason. But it is altogether different to suggest that the sum of all these symbols adds up to eternal and pointless torture at the hands of a sadistic God.

These are symbols that should call us to sobriety and reflection on our current lives and the very real consequences of our thoughts and deeds. They speak of a God who understands the seriousness of what we do and don't do far better than our shortsighted minds can comprehend. Does *Gehenna* speak of some sort of punishment after death? Yes, I think so. Yet we have no reason to believe such punishment will be perpetual torture, without the possibility of repentance or reform. After all, the same Christ who invoked *Gehenna* as a symbol of judgment is the same one who said, "I do not judge anyone who hears my words and does not keep them, for I came not to judge the world but to save the world" (John 12:47) and "indeed, God did not send the Son into the world to condemn the world but in order that the world might be saved through him" (John 3:17).

Therein lies the problem. It's obvious that Christians are willing to work very hard to find (or even construct) an eternal hell within the pages of the Bible. We are all too willing to pull, stretch, and generally contort ancient words and images that fit a certain paradigm of eternal doom, but we aren't nearly as willing to do the same for those scriptures that speak to the infinite love and compassion of God. In that way, hell isn't merely a doctrine or a dogma that we believe. It has become a lens by which we have come to interpret the Bible and relate to our God.

When it comes to forgiveness, our first instinct is to set a limit and draw a boundary that even God cannot cross. Surely, there must be *some* who are beyond the love of Christ, some who must be damned, some who are destined to suffer for the sins of the world. As if to say that surely, not even God can go an eternity without being cruel to *someone*.

Of course, God's mercy is not bound by our pitiful imagination. That should have been made clear to us when Jesus, hanging from the cross, looked down at the Roman soldiers, the Judean leaders, and the disciples who betrayed him and said, "Father, forgive them, for they know not what they do" (Luke 23:34 ESV).

What sin could be more damnable than the murder of God's only begotten Son? What crimes could compare to crying out for his death, driving the nails into his wrists, mocking his pain, and then abandoning him to his cross? Yet at that very moment, with his last few breaths, Christ proclaimed their forgiveness—even as they were still murdering him.

Why hasn't this become the lens by which we interpret everything the Bible has to say about the afterlife rather than pagan myths that we don't even understand? Why doesn't the immensity of God's grace capture our imaginations in the same way as eternal divine vengeance? Why do we work so hard to defend the idea that in order for the gospel to be "good news" for us, it must be a curse for others?

One wonders if there isn't some part of us, deep down, that wants God to be cruel, perhaps as if to excuse our own penchant toward cruelty.

The truth is that hell has become vital to the functioning of most forms of Christianity. For some Christians, it has become as theologically important as the incarnation, the cross, or the resurrection. That is why it is defended so vociferously and why I will be labeled a heretic for writing this book. Over the centuries, hell has developed into a kind of linchpin upon which the entire infrastructure of Christian doctrine has been made to rest—an eternal torment that balances out infinite love, an infernal yang to the gospel yin, the ultimate stick of divine sadism that off-sets the carrot of compassion and forgiveness. To question the damnation of lost souls has become, in effect, to question the very thing that makes Christianity tolerable to contemporary Christians—that there will ultimately be sheep and goats, wheat and tares, lives that are of infinite eternal value and lives that are eternally worthless.

My fear is that for some of us, that dichotomy is all that makes Christianity worth believing.

four

a paddle in the hands
of an angry god

About every five hundred years the empowered structures of institutionalized Christianity . . . become an
intolerable carapace that must be shattered in order that
renewal and new growth may occur.

—Phyllis Tickle, *The Great Emergence*

When I was a child, the scariest place in my home wasn't the
basement or the attic. I was never afraid of what terrible
creature might lie behind the furnace or dwell deep in the bowels
of the crawlspace. No, the most terrifying part of my house, of my
whole world for that matter, was the wall just above the kitchen
sink. I was scared of it because on that wall was a nail, and on that
nail hung a small, innocuous-looking piece of wood with a flower
painted on it. It was my mother's paddle.

Truth be told, I don't think I ever "got the paddle." It was never
moved down from that nail to be used for its intended purpose,
but that didn't matter. It was all about the threat of the thing, the
idea that if I ever let my behavior get too far out of control, that if
I ever crossed some unstated boundary, it could be taken down

and brought to bear against my backside. On more than one oc-
casion, all my mom had to do was look in its general direction and
I would be magically transformed from a snotty little kid into an
absolute cherub. It was the mere specter of the paddle that kept
me in line.

I think some of us imagine that God's punishment works like
that paddle, that hell is this ongoing threat of retribution that is
supposed to drive us to have faith in Jesus and, once such faith is
declared, to keep us walking "the straight and narrow." Yet in order
for such a threat to be as effective as possible, it seems we made
it as severe as possible—even to the point of imagining the *most*
severe thing possible—in order to keep an ever-present reminder
hanging over our heads, so we always remember what's at stake.
Because of that, some folks come to depend on that paddle in order to make sense of the world. They may even come to love it.

I remember this man who came to visit my church one Sunday. He didn't look very happy. He just sat there through the
whole service in the back pew with his arms folded, staring a hole
through the back of my head. He didn't get up for the passing of
the peace. He didn't budge for Communion. After the final blessing, I moved to the back of the sanctuary to start shaking hands.
Eventually he moseyed on up to me, his arms still crossed, and
asked, "Y'all preach hell in here?"

I was taken off guard by the question. "I'm sorry, what?"

This good ol' boy spoke a bit louder. "Y'all preach hellfire in
here, or y'all got that 'feel-good' gospel?" He ended his question
with a mocking sneer.

I sensed in his voice that the answer he was looking for was
something like "You bet your ass we preach hell!" That confused me because it seemed as if this ostensibly Christian man
was looking for a church that would warn him about hell on a
weekly basis.

All I could muster was, "Well, um . . . we preach the good news
of forgiveness of sin in Jesus Christ."

"Yeah . . ." he said while shaking his head, "that's 'bout what I thought." He turned and left without saying goodbye and didn't ever come back.

Our relationship with hell is complicated. On one hand, hell is literally the worst thing in the world that we all hope to avoid. On the other, some of us look at it with something like nostalgic affection. For some, hell is like that tiny, terrible paddle: the instrument by which we started acting right, the threat we needed to get our lives in order. It's hard to imagine life without it being there, hovering on the wall just over our heads, a stationary menace that we think helps to keep our darkest impulses in check and our feet walking the straight and narrow path. We wonder, If we take that paddle down, would we start to wander? Would the church even continue to exist? What might happen to our civilization if the threat of ultimate destruction were taken off the table?

As we unwind the unbiblical myth of eternal torment, we need to interrogate just what punishment is, how it works, and how it's supposed to work.

st. anselm's fire

Like I said, I don't remember my mom ever using the paddle to punish me, but I was spanked as a kid. It was usually with a hand to the bottom, never leaving a mark or a bruise, and it was often accompanied by the assurance, "This hurts me more than it hurts you."

I don't have children, so I don't know a lot about raising a child. I do know that there are many parents who have very passionate opinions about corporal punishment, both those who think it is an indispensable tool of discipline and those who think it is downright evil. I have no desire to speak to that debate. What I hope we can all agree with is the idea that corporal punishment *can* cross a boundary, that there's a point at which striking a child transgresses a sacred line—the line between restoration and retribution, between shaping a child's character and crushing a child's will. One of the things our society has started to understand in the last century is that we have to be careful with such punishment, because when it becomes more about the wrath of the parent than about the education of the child, discipline gives way to abuse.

I was one of the lucky ones. When I was spanked, I somehow knew it wasn't abuse. It didn't seem arbitrary or grounded in malice. I understood that my mother never meant it for evil. She thought I needed that little jolt of pain in order to punctuate a lesson I was too stubborn to learn. Even if I wouldn't have said it at the time, I got the point that it was for my own good. Someplace deep down I knew that the punishment I received from my mother was on the *restorative* side of the line.

If everything we call hell is some kind of punishment from God, then on which side of that line does it lie? Does God punish in order to execute vengeance or does God punish in order to teach and restore?

For a man named Anselm of Canterbury, it was definitely the former. Anselm was a medieval theologian whose ideas shaped how Christians have thought about hell for centuries. In his most famous work, *Cur Deus Homo* (sometimes translated as *Why the God Man?* or *Why Did God Become Man?*), Anselm argued not only that God must punish, but that God must punish *infinitely.*

To understand his argument, you have to understand something about Anselm's world. The Middle Ages were a time of honor. Today, we talk about honor in the abstract, but for those in medieval Europe, honor was much more concrete, almost tangible. It was a period when society was ruled by the strict social hierarchy of feudalism, when vassals were expected to serve their lords and subjects were bound to obey their kings. To disobey someone higher on the ladder than you was to dishonor that person, to almost literally steal their honor, and the penalty for such a crime was dependent on the status of the victim. Steal food from another poor peasant, and you might get a slap on the wrist. Steal food from the table of your lord, and you might just lose your hand. Steal from a king, and you would surely lose your life.

For Anselm, God was the highest Lord, and therefore, God was owed infinite honor. To sin against such a Lord was an infinite crime that required an infinite punishment: eternal hell. It was not even that God could *choose* to punish someone eternally; it was that God was honor-bound to do it. God's own justice demanded eternal and infinite retribution. God literally had no choice but to collect on this debt of honor, and we, being finite mortals, could never hope to pay.

However, Anselm did believe that God created a loophole, and his name was Jesus. God offered God's own Son in the person of Jesus Christ to suffer death and to vicariously absorb the wrath of God's justice on behalf of those who believed in him. Meanwhile, of course, the rest of humanity would be resigned to hell, which for Anselm was a kind of debtors prison where souls would spend an eternity of torment never quite paying off their debt of honor.

At the time, such logic made perfect sense, both socially and theologically. The authority of your local lord came from the king, whose authority, in turn, came from God. If God was the King of kings and the Lord of lords, then he had the Honor of all honors, and the besmirching of God's infinite name required an infinite price. Divine justice demanded it.

That's how the doctrine of eternal torment grounded medieval society and why the Middle Ages are the one period of history in which we see a curious absence of those who oppose it.[1] God's violence against humanity anchored the authority of lords and kings to threaten violence against their own people. To question the threat of eternal torture would have been to question the legitimacy of torture in the temporal realm.

Thankfully we no longer tend to think about life and society in terms of honor (except perhaps in the military), but if you've spent much time in church, this should still sound familiar. Anselm was a monumental influence on the Roman Catholic Church as well as the likes of Martin Luther, John Calvin, and John Wesley. His interpretation has shaped the theology of Catholics, evangelicals, and mainline Protestants alike, even to this day. Whenever the sacrifice of Jesus is put in terms of a transaction, when the cross of Christ becomes a kind of shield that defends us from the wrath of God, that's the influence of Anselm. Whenever you hear a sermon or a worship song that speaks of Jesus "taking my place" or "paying my debt," that's Anselm peeking out through the centuries.

Reading Anselm in the twenty-first century, I have some questions. Why does God need to defend God's honor? Why would God be bound to punish? What force in the universe would compel God to do that? Why is it that the only two things in the universe that can satisfy this debt are either the death of God incarnate or eternal punishment? If the requirements of something called "divine justice" can put such restraints on God, then shouldn't we be worshiping that instead?

the church of fatal attraction

It seems to me that, for as much as we Christians like to talk about God's forgiveness and love for humanity, we spend a lot of time telling people that they need to be saved—not from the devil, mind you, but from God. In the grand scheme of Anselmian Christianity, God is the real threat. God is the one who judges, who casts the verdict and executes the sentence. If hell is anything, it's a kitchen paddle in the hands of God.

Consider these lines from one of the most famous sermons from one of the most influential preachers in all of American history, Jonathan Edwards:

The God that holds you over the pit of Hell, much as one holds a spider or some loathsome insect over the fire, abhors you, and is dreadfully provoked; his wrath towards you burns like fire; he looks upon you as worthy of nothing else, but to be cast into the fire . . . you are ten thousand times so abominable in his eyes, as the most hateful and venomous serpent is in ours.[2]

Edwards was the father of the First Great Awakening, the spiritual movement that fueled the rise of evangelicalism and set the religious tone of the thirteen colonies that would eventually become the United States. The words of his famous sermon, "Sinners in the Hands of an Angry God," baptized America.

But this theology, this style of preaching, this whole system of understanding our relationship to God is not some relic of the long-lost past. It continues to thrive even today: "God hates, right now, personally, objectively, some of you. . . . Some of you, God hates you. . . . Some of you, God is sick of you. God is frustrated with you. God has suffered long enough with you."[3]

This sermon didn't come from some backwater snake-handling church or some doomsday cult from the periphery of the Bible Belt. No, that gem of a homily was given in 2011 by Mark Driscoll, a Seattle-area pastor who, at the time, was one of the most popular and best-selling preachers in America. The main thrust of his message that day was that human sin has offended God to such a degree that the infinitely perfect Jesus had to come to earth to stand in the way of God's righteous vengeance. Preachers like Driscoll like to say that Jesus saves us from sin, but really that's only true insofar as Jesus saves us from the damnation that God seeks to impose on us for our sin. God is still the ultimate source of the wrath.

There are quite a few who make their stock and trade preaching these kinds of sermons, but in most churches, you won't hear anything like Driscoll's blunt declaration of God's hatred. That kind of "fire and brimstone" doesn't go down quite so well among the majority of Christians. However, if you're paying attention, you start to see it everywhere, even in the most caring and hospitable congregations. One can almost always detect a subtle unwillingness to question the idea of hell lurking just behind all the sermons about divine mercy and forgiveness—an assurance that, no matter how good we make God sound, the threat of eternal torture will never go away.

For instance, in the middle of a sermon or a Bible study, just as the speaker is starting to emphasize God's love or forgiveness, have you ever been reminded to "balance God's love with God's justice"? Have you ever been told to recall that the humble Jesus of Nazareth was also the sword-waving, world-conquering Christ of Revelation, the human incarnation of the same God who cursed Sodom and Gomorrah? Has anyone ever felt it was necessary to warn you against believing in a "limp-wristed," hippy snowflake Jesus?[4]

I've found that some, if not most, preachers feel that they need to drop such reminders from the pulpit when their words about the love of God become too powerful, when the scope of the divine forgiveness becomes too grand, when God starts to sound somehow too merciful.

There remains a part of us that wants to hang on to that idea of hell, that *wants* to imagine that God not only punishes, but punishes for the sake of eternal vengeance. Maybe it's because somewhere deep down we think that's the only thing keeping us in line, that keeps us from going down a darker path. Maybe we think that such threats are the only thing that keeps the world together, that if we remove the threat of divine wrath, civilization itself might fall apart. The sad point is that most of us will never know why we seem so connected to the idea of hell because the moment we start to interrogate that belief, some priest or pastor comes along to offer us those wonderful words of assurance: "Don't worry. God still damns."

In the most subtle of ways, the message from the church is always clear: we can talk about forgiveness and salvation and mercy, but we must never abandon the idea of eternal punishment altogether. We will never make you imagine a world without the threat of hell. You can always take comfort in the fact that God loves you and wants a personal relationship with you . . . but also won't hesitate to turn around and torture you forever if you reject him.

This should sound familiar if you've ever seen the 1987 thriller *Fatal Attraction*. The main character is a married man who has a one-night stand with a woman. She wants to turn their fling into a relationship, but he thinks better of it, rejecting her offer and deciding instead to stay with his wife and daughter. All should be well, except that the jilted mistress continues to love the cheating husband so much that she actually hurts herself, then she threatens his family, and finally she ultimately tries to kill the man she supposedly *loves*. If she can't have him, no one will. The movie is enthralling precisely because it confronts us with a character whose "love" is supposedly so great that it turns into murderous wrath, and the crazy part is that on some level, we can relate to it. The movie is powerful because it exposes a contradiction that lies very deep within the human heart, where the line between love and hate can be thin and faint, and we can often feel as if we burn with both at the same time.

Just think about the way those closest to us can elicit such powerful feelings on both sides of that spectrum. Those of us who are married know that we love that one special person more than anything else in the whole world—and we also know that no one else can drive us up the wall quite like they can. We would die for our children, but they also make us want to pull out our hair. On some level, we all feel that contradiction, that emotional tension that lives inside of us. If it's not handled appropriately, that tension can turn otherwise loving relationships into sources of dysfunction and pain.

Maybe that's why some of us feel that on some level, God *must* hate us, at least to some degree. Surely, we think, God must be as conflicted as we are. If God loves so deeply, then somewhere God must also burn with a matching depth of hatred.

As sacrilegious as it is, we hang on to hell because we want God to be just like us.

our deadbeat dad, who art in heaven

The problem with believing in a God who hates us, of course, is that Jesus told us something else entirely: "Is there anyone among you who, if your child asked for bread, would give a stone? Or if the child asked for a fish, would give a snake? If you, then, who are evil, know how to give good gifts to your children, how much more will *your* Father in heaven give good things to those who ask him!" (Matt. 7:9–11, emphasis mine).

What I always have to remember about this passage is Jesus's use of the word "your." For all the talk we have about Jesus being "the Son of God" and "God the Son," I can get caught up in the idea that God is only his father, that Jesus has some exclusive kind of relationship to God that I could never hope to access. But when it comes down to it, Jesus keeps using that "your" to try to remind us that God is our Father too and that we have a Father who only wants good things for us.

If God is our Father, our Parent, the one who takes a kind of ultimate responsibility for us, then whatever discipline God has for us must be at least *akin* to the kind of punishment a loving parent would have for their child. We can certainly disagree on the issue of whether parents should strike their children, but isn't there something that is undoubtedly abusive about a parent who refuses to hold their children accountable for their actions? Discipline, boundaries, consequences, character formation—these are all part of what it means to be a parent. If someone refuses to take responsibility for the formation of a child's character, can that person be considered a parent at all?

Likewise, if a parent only punishes a child, if constant punishment is the sole means by which a person relates to their own child, would we still rightly call that person a parent? If the entire

relationship is reduced to nothing but a torrent of wrath endlessly flowing from the greater to the lesser (as the doctrine of
hell seems to indicate), then terms like Father, Mother, or Parent
would mean nothing except to highlight that God abuses some
of God's children but not others.

Matthew 7:9–11 is part of the Sermon on the Mount, a speech
that Jesus gave to a crowd gathered from all around the Judean
countryside. Matthew goes out of his way to mention that the
people there came from Galilee, Jerusalem, and even a place called
the Decapolis (Matt. 4:25). To modern readers, that doesn't mean
much, and so we just assume that Jesus was talking to fellow Jews,
telling them about *their* Father. But the Decapolis was a league of
Roman cities in Judea, cities where they paid no homage to Yah-
weh, where they worshiped the gods of the Roman pantheon.

Matthew is trying to tell us that the "your" of Jesus's message
wasn't only for Jews, members of a chosen religion, but that it
also included pagan gentiles. Jesus's Father is the Father of Jew
and gentile alike. Of course, it wasn't just that the Romans didn't
worship God. They were also an occupying force in Israel. They
were political enemies, even oppressors to the Jews. Yet Jesus ad-
dresses them all as a single human family:

> You have heard that it was said, "You shall love your neighbor
> and hate your enemy." But I say to you: Love your enemies
> and pray for those who persecute you, so that you may be
> children of your Father in heaven, for he makes his sun rise
> on the evil and on the good and sends rain on the righteous
> and on the unrighteous. For if you love those who love you,
> what reward do you have? Do not even the tax collectors do
> the same? . . . Be perfect, therefore, as your heavenly Father
> is perfect. (Matt. 5:43–48)

Notice how Jesus anchors this teaching at the end of the passage.
He doesn't tell us to love our enemies because it's the right thing to

do or because it leads to a happier life (as true as those things might be). Rather, he appeals to the fact that we are children of a common Father. Retribution is simply not in our DNA. An "eye for an eye" is not part of our family culture. Despite what we may have heard from earlier stories and scriptures, it is not something we inherited from our divine Parent. In fact, the opposite is true. We are to love our enemies because God loves God's enemies. We are not to repay evil for evil because God does not repay evil for evil. We are to forgive because forgiveness is the way of our family.

If Jesus really thought that God plunged God's enemies into a hell of eternal torture, then how would this teaching make sense? How could Jesus tell us to love our enemies in imitation of God, if God doesn't also love God's enemies?

I understand that sometimes love has to feel harsh. Sometimes we have to force our children to take that yucky medicine or douse their cuts with that stinging spray. Sometimes we have to confront loved ones, put up boundaries, and execute consequences for bad behavior. But I simply find it unfathomable to say that it is possible to love someone while simultaneously torturing that person *for all eternity*. That's a snake that no parent would ever hand their child.

The cousin I mentioned in the first chapter (the one who told me in misplaced confidence that he no longer believed in God) actually went down a very dark path in life. He has been in prison for over thirty years for committing a grizzly murder. I've spoken on the phone with him a handful of times, but I've never gone to see him in the penitentiary. I'd like to catch up with him someday and find out how he's really been doing all these years, but I've kept our conversations brief. I guess I've never quite known how to talk to a member of my family who did something so terrible.

His mother, on the other hand, has never been so double-minded. After all this time, she still goes to visit him, celebrates his birthday, and makes sure he's getting enough to eat. She has no illusions about the gravity of his crimes, and I don't think any one of us would have blamed her for cutting him out of her life and letting him rot in prison. But that isn't what a mother does. No, she waits with eager anticipation for the day her son can come back home.

If she who is fallen, conflicted, and sinful could exhibit such patience and tenderness toward a child who has hurt her so badly, how much more patience and kindness will our Father show to us? Should we believe that such compassion actually constitutes some kind of weakness on her part? Is God more holy than my aunt because God is less compassionate? Or have we spent too much time convincing ourselves that God isn't a Father after all?

I think there is a simple question we should ask folks like Anselm, Driscoll, and all those preachers who always feel that they have to point to the hell paddle on the wall: Does God actually forgive sins or not? In nearly every church around the globe, we Christians gladly preach the gospel of the forgiveness of sins, yet if Jesus's role is simply to absorb the wrath of the Father in our place, then that gospel is a lie. The sin hasn't been forgiven at all. The debt has not been canceled. The sentence has not been lifted, only transferred to an innocent party—a divine sibling who has thrown himself into the path of a Father who punishes with abusive vengeance.

the five-hundred-year rummage sale

As I grew up, that old paddle seemed to fade away. It continued to hang up on that nail for years, same as it ever had, but as I grew into the person my mother and father shaped me to become, it fell off the radar of my mind. I no longer needed that kind of threat in order to do the right thing.

A couple years ago, my parents wanted to sell the house of my childhood and move into someplace a little smaller and more manageable. So they did what most people do: they went through all their old stuff, put up a few card tables in the garage, and had themselves a rummage sale.

I happened to stop by when my dad was setting it up. When I saw the paddle just sitting there with a sticker that read "25¢,"

I picked it up. A smile stretched across my face because I couldn't believe how thin and flimsy it was. To my young mind, it was some kind of medieval melee weapon, but as I held it in my adult hands and beheld it in my mature heart, I realized there was never anything to be scared of.

I brought it inside to show my mom. We shared a laugh and reminisced for a bit about some of my "behavioral challenges" as a kid, but then she suddenly got very serious. "I just want to say that I'm sorry about that," she said.

"Mom, it was fine. It's not like you were abusive. You never even used it on me," I tried to reassure her.

"No. You were good kids, and sometimes I was too tough on you. I never meant to frighten you. I'm sorry."

I couldn't help but start to cry.

Phyllis Tickle likes to say that about once every five hundred years the church likes to go through all its old stuff and hold a rummage sale.[5] Every so often, it seems as if we need a reformation or a schism or the fall of an empire to push us off the sofa, get us up to the attic, and force us to start cleaning out all the things we've collected over the years. Sometimes, in the midst of all that conflict and upheaval, we find some long-lost treasure, and we put it back on the mantel. Other times, it's Dad's neon Coors sign, or a musty old blanket, or even a silly little paddle. That's the stuff we used to love, the stuff that may have served us well at some point, but its time in our lives is over.

There have been many good, even saintly, Christians who came to the faith through the fear of hell. It has helped folks get right with God, healed their relationships, and kept them away from the sins that may have destroyed their lives. And just like that old neon sign, it might still even work! But there comes a time to look at old things with new eyes and start to see that our Parent never meant us any harm.

five

breaking out of baby jail

Can a woman forget her nursing child or show no compassion for the child of her womb? Even these might forget, yet I will not forget you.

—Isaiah 49:15

There aren't very many Sunday school lessons that I can actually remember from my childhood, but there is one that, for some reason, I've never forgotten. It was about three men (memorably named Shadrach, Meshach, and Abednego) who refused to bow down and pay homage to King Nebuchadnezzar's golden statue. Perhaps you remember the story: the king had them thrown into a fiery furnace. I can still clearly recall seeing the three men stuck to a green felt board while my Sunday school teacher added strip after strip of bright orange fabric to the scene as she explained that the evil king ordered the furnace to be stoked to *seven* times its normal temperature. Yet the men were unharmed, and my teacher added one more figure to the board. It was Jesus!

Now, truth be told, my Sunday school teacher took some theological liberties with that last bit. There's nothing in the text that says definitively the fourth figure in the fire was the preincarnate Jesus, though Nebuchadnezzar does say, "and the appearance of the fourth is like a son of the gods" (Dan. 3:25 ESV).

Nevertheless, I got the point I think I was supposed to get. God didn't keep Shadrach, Meshach, and Abednego from the furnace. He didn't stop them from getting into trouble nor did he pull them out from the fire. What God did do was go down into the furnace with them and dwell in the flames.

left to rot

I got a lot of mileage out of that story when I interned as a chaplain at a youth detention facility for boys. It seemed to resonate with those who found themselves trapped in a difficult place. The "youth detention facility" was what people used to call a "juvenile hall," but the inmates affectionately referred to it as "baby jail." Baby jail, despite the name, was its own kind of furnace, full of tough kids and tough guards keeping them in line. Even the physical environment was harsh. There were almost no soft surfaces. For the sake of cleanliness everything had to be hard and waterproof. The air was always hot and humid, and every room reeked of bleach because blood and other bodily fluids often made their way to the cinderblock walls or the hard linoleum floors. Someone somewhere was always yelling or crying, and suicide was a daily concern, as was sexual abuse among inmates.

When I spoke to the kids there, they talked as if they always wanted God to deliver them from their circumstances in some kind of miraculous way. They wanted God to get them out, to fix their lives and make them happy, and they wanted to know why God wasn't helping their broken families back home. In a word, they wanted to know why bad things happen and why they don't seem to be getting any better. Most of the time the only answer I had for them was to tell the story of Shadrach, Meshach, and Abednego and explain as well as I could that no matter how difficult the situation, God was in the furnace with them.

The interesting thing was that you never really knew how long one of the kids would be held in baby jail. At that particular time and in that particular state, the law was such that judges could not hand down fixed-term sentences to juvenile offenders. They weren't allowed to set a number of months or years in advance that the offender would have to stay; rather, the length of one's term in detention was determined by the progress one made toward rehabilitation.

Each inmate was assigned a team made up of teachers, counselors, doctors, and other professionals who would meet a few times a year, assess how he was doing, and make a recommendation to the judge. If the kid was getting into fights, failing in his schoolwork, or not taking his counseling seriously, he would have to stay, and the team would do another assessment in a few months. If the kid met certain benchmarks, he could be released into the custody of a parent or guardian.

At the time, I actually felt that this was a great policy. It was organized to keep kids in the system only as long as they needed to be there. It seemed to incentivize the kids to work toward their own rehabilitation and restoration, exactly the kind of discipline one would want to see when children were involved. Along with that policy, the teams could build individualized plans based on each child's particular needs and situation. The system seemed compassionate, humane, and responsible. The only problem was that the policy assumed that every rehabilitated child had someplace to go and someone who wanted to come get them.

During my time teaching Bible study and leading worship services in baby jail, there was one particular student I would watch out of the corner of my eye. We'll call him Darrell. Darrell was a very large seventeen-year-old with a perpetual scowl on his face. He was quiet, even sullen, unless he was yelling at the staff or his fellow inmates. He got into lots of fights, some of them bloody, and often had to be removed from the general population. Even though he didn't want anything to do with church or prayer or anything like that, I always knew exactly where Darrell was when I was on his unit. More than any other kid, he made me nervous.

But I came to find out that he wasn't always like that. As it turned out, Darrell had been in baby jail since he was eleven. When he first got there, he got along well with everyone. He was polite and motivated. He worked hard at his studies, took his medicine, and cooperated with his counselors—all this without ever getting a single visitor from home. Neither his mom nor dad nor anyone else ever came to see to Darrell, but he kept doing the work. He did so well that he met all his criteria for release in just one year! But when it came time for him to be sent home, his parents simply refused to come get him. In other words, his own family left him to rot. Without a parent or a guardian to take custody of Darrell, the state couldn't just release a minor out into the community. They had no choice but to keep him there until someone picked him up or he aged out of the system.

As he sat there, month after month, during the most formative time of his life, watching friends come and go, Darrell understandably started to disintegrate. As the seasons turned and the calendar pages fell, he became more stubborn and angry. He started lashing out, throwing punches, and cussing at the staff. Eventually he stopped doing his schoolwork altogether, refused to meet with his counselor, and even attempted suicide by setting his own bed on fire. By the time I met him, he was a burnt-out husk of a child, charred by seven years of sitting in that furnace all by himself. Reformed or not, that baby jail was Darrell's world until his eighteenth birthday, when the state authorities would give him twenty-five dollars and a bus ticket and send him on his way.

Remember how I mentioned the impossibility of true hopelessness? Darrell probably came closer than anyone I've ever met, but it wasn't because he was somehow incapable of redemption or rehabilitation. It was because the people in his life who were supposed to love him most, the ones he was supposed to call "mother" and "father," simply refused to come and bring him home.

the meaning of "all"

Any belief that God would leave even one beloved child to suffer in some kind of endless fiery prison offends everything Christ taught us about the nature of God. Some people believe in an eternal hell because they think the Bible teaches it. What they fail to see is that an everlasting hell contradicts the entire overarching narrative of the Bible itself.

In our vaguely Christian American culture, I think most church folks imagine that the Scriptures make up some kind of grand story, the climax of which is them going *up* to heaven and all the bad people going *down* to hell. That is the point of everything, isn't it? At the end of the day, after all the Scriptures are read and the prayers are prayed and the bread is dipped in the wine, most people just want to know that they're going to escape the "lake of fire" and that they're going to see their loved ones behind the "pearly gates."

If that is what some, if not most, people think, then we preachers have not done a very good job over the years. In fact, I would say that we've failed at telling the church's story, because that story is not about us going up. It's about God coming *down*. Consider all the stories you remember from the Bible:

God comes down to the earth and walks in the cool of the day (Gen. 3:8).

God comes down and wrestles Jacob by the shore of the Jabbock River (Gen. 32:22–32).

God comes down in the form of the burning bush, saves Israel from Egypt, and gives the law to Moses at Sinai (Exod. 20).

God comes down and speaks through the prophets (2 Sam. 23:2).

God comes down in the fire of the Holy Spirit at Pentecost (Acts 2).

Even the very incarnation we celebrate by singing "Love Came Down at Christmas" testifies to the fact that we have a God who comes down to us. The birth of Christ reveals to us that God refuses to abandon us. God refuses to simply let us lie in our own filth or stew in our own resentment until we become burnt-out husks of the people we were created to be. The very life of Christ teaches us that no matter how far down we go, God will follow us there.

Paul beautifully quotes a first-century hymn to this "coming down" of Christ in the Letter to the Philippians, where he speaks of Jesus emptying himself, taking on the form of a slave, and embracing all the humility of human life, even death on the cross (Phil. 2:6–8). The purpose of this divine descent into the darkness of the world, Paul declares, is "so that at the name given to Jesus every knee should bend, in heaven and on earth and *under the earth*, and every tongue should confess that Jesus Christ is Lord, to the glory of God the Father" (Phil. 2:10–11, emphasis mine).

If you are tempted to think that those who are "under the earth" will make their confession through gritted teeth and the bitter pain of torment, allow me to remind you that the same Paul who wrote this passage from Philippians also wrote that "no one can say 'Jesus is Lord' except by the Holy Spirit" (1 Cor. 12:3).

This closely mirrors what Paul quotes in Romans: "As I live, says the Lord, every knee shall bow to me, and every tongue shall give praise to God" (Rom. 14:11). Again, we might imagine that Paul is speaking of some kind of *forced* confession here, that he's trying to say, "God is so glorious that even those who burn for all eternity will still be compelled to bend the knee to God."

The thing is, that's not how defeat usually works. It's not often that conquered enemies actually come to *praise* their conquerors (especially if their conquerors continue to torture them), and if they do, why would they still be considered enemies?[1] That would be like Darrell praising his absentee parents who continued to leave him to rot in prison. Are we to believe that Paul is trying to describe a hell that is full of those who praise and submit to

God yet nevertheless continue to burn? That doesn't sound very glorious at all. In fact, it feels kind of sadistic. Wouldn't it make more sense to take a moment and bracket everything we've been told about a hell of eternal torment and admit that it's more likely that Paul is saying that, given enough time, everyone will come around to God eventually? Wouldn't it make more sense to believe that verses like these are grounded in the idea that given enough time, God wins *every* soul? Or is that just a little too . . . *universalist*? (There, I finally said it.)

This certainly wouldn't be the only place where Paul seems to say that God's salvation is *universal* in nature. For instance, modern-day evangelists love to remind us that "all have sinned and fall short of the glory of God" as proof that sin and guilt are the lone traits that are universal among humankind, but they often leave out the rest of the sentence: "For there is no distinction, since all have sinned and fall short of the glory of God; they are now justified by his grace as a gift, through the redemption that is in Jesus Christ" (Rom. 3:22–24). By the logic of this sentence, the pronoun "they" in the second clause refers to the "all" in the first. It's true that "all" have certainly sinned and fall short, but "all" have also been justified and redeemed.

In fact, I would say that the word "all" is one of Paul's favorite words to use when discussing the scope of salvation. To the church in Rome he says, "Therefore just as one man's [Adam's] trespass led to condemnation for *all*, so one man's [Christ's] act of righteousness leads to justification and life for *all*" (Rom. 5:18, emphasis mine) and, "For God has imprisoned *all* in disobedience so that he may be merciful to *all*" (Rom. 11:32, emphasis mine).

Paul's theme of universal salvation isn't confined merely to the book of Romans; in 1 Corinthians we have, "for as *all* die in Adam, so *all* will be made alive in Christ" (1 Cor. 15:22, emphasis mine). And let us not forget Paul's words in the Letter to Titus: "For the grace of God has appeared, bringing salvation to *all*" (Titus 2:11, emphasis mine).

Now I don't mean to start some kind of prooftexting war, as if arguing over theology were just a matter of slapping more verses down on the table than the other guy. I admit that one can seem to find an eternity of pain and abandonment all over the Bible—if that's what one is looking for. And I suppose there are some evangelicals who would happily squint their eyes and apply some kind of strained interpretation to the verses I quote above to make the case that "all" never actually means "all" when talking about salvation. I used to do the same thing myself. But after years studying the Bible and the traditions of Christianity, I've finally given up. At some point, Christians have to stop defending the indefensible and accept the very thing that Christ came to earth to teach us: that God will always come down to us. God will never leave us abandoned. God will never leave us to face the darkness alone, no matter how deep it may be. At some point, we have to admit that, like it or not, "neither death, nor life, nor angels, nor rulers, nor things present, nor things to come, nor powers, nor height, nor depth, nor anything else in all creation will be able to separate us from the love of God in Christ Jesus our Lord" (Rom. 8:38–39).

refiner's fire

There's one more instance of this divine descent that we need to discuss. In Revelation 21, we see God *coming down* once again, this time with a new heaven and a new earth in tow. Again, notice that the story of Revelation ends not with us climbing or even floating up to God in heaven but with God and heaven coming down to us, so that "the home of God is among mortals. He will dwell with them; they will be his peoples, and God himself will be with them and be their God; he will wipe every tear from their eyes" (Rev. 21:3–4).

But the picture is far from perfect: "for the cowardly, the faithless, the polluted, the murderers, the sexually immoral, the sorcerers, the idolaters, and all liars, their place will be in the lake that burns with fire and sulfur, which is the second death" (Rev. 21:8).

Surely this must be a reference to a hell of eternal torment, right? It's all right there: bad people, a lake, and even the famous "fire and brimstone," the latter being another name for sulfur.

How often have we heard that term "fire and brimstone" applied to any judgmental preacher who typically or even enthusiastically talks about hell? It has become so common and overused that few of us really know what it means anymore. Yet any goldsmith or metallurgist worth their salt would know immediately what the term means and why it has nothing to do with eternal torture.

"Fire and brimstone" is an idiom that refers to purification. To be exact, it references the refinement of gold or other precious metals. Most precious metals don't come in nice little globs that can be plucked from the ground, washed off, and immediately turned into coins or jewelry. Metal usually comes in the form of ore that is loaded with all kinds of impurities, other rocks, and minerals that surround and cover up the metal you're trying to get. If the metal is to be useful, it must be purified. It has to be separated from the ore around it. In a word, it must be refined.

If one is trying to refine gold, for instance, it must be melted down into a bright orange pool of molten ore. (In Greek, the word for a "pool of molten metal," *limnē*, just happens to be the same word that is translated as "lake" in the passage.) Then powdered sulfur is added to it, making flames shoot out from the glowing-hot lake. In the midst of the resulting fire, the sulfur binds to all the impurities within the gold to make light, chalky sulfides that rise to the top as slag to be scooped out and disposed of, leaving behind only the pure, valuable gold.

This passage near the end of Revelation continues a theme from all the way back in the words of the prophet Malachi: "But who can endure the day of his coming, and who can stand when he appears? For he is like a refiner's fire and like washers' soap; he will sit as a refiner and purifier of silver, and he will purify the descendants of Levi and refine them like gold and silver, until they present offerings to the Lord in righteousness" (Mal. 3:2–3).

The lake of fire and brimstone, the "second death," is not eternal agony or even a kind of final annihilation as some believe, as if God will finally eradicate the souls of sinners in an ultimate fiery blast of divine wrath. Rather, in Revelation 21, we witness the final death of all that is dark and impure within *us*. Unlike Malachi's prophecy, this refiner's fire isn't just for the descendants of Levi; it's for all the dross of humanity, all the sin and vice and selfishness that stain our hearts and separate us from God and one another. Hell, if it is anything, is a fiery furnace where all that is impure and unworthy is finally scorched away (some might even say *purged*) from humanity until only the pure and unadulterated image of God is left.[2] And if that's true, and if, like Shadrach, Meshach, Abednego, we find ourselves cast into the flames, we can be sure that one "like a son of the gods" will be there with us, until the time comes to take us home (Dan. 3:8–25 ESV).

christ's commando raid on hell

Have you ever heard of the "Harrowing of Hell"? You shouldn't feel bad if you haven't because most American Christians don't talk about it much these days. Eastern Orthodox and Roman Catholic Churches still consider it to be an important article of faith, but my experience is that most of the folks in their pews haven't heard of it. The Harrowing is even less well known to mainline Protestants, and most evangelical preachers would probably consider it to be some kind of heresy. Yet even among these last two groups, it still pops up from time to time. For instance, those who come from churches that regularly recite the Apostles' Creed might recognize the line "he descended into hell" (or sometimes it reads, "into Hades" or "to the dead"). This is a reference to the Harrowing of Hell.

Even though it almost never comes up in Bible study and most of us have never heard it mentioned in a sermon, this descent into the underworld used to be a very big deal to Christians.

A harrow is a heavy rake that is used to "distress" a field. A farmer drags it over their soil to break up the dirt and remove any rocks or roots that might get in the way of the plow. Some people use harrows to glean, to pick up any produce that the harvest left behind. "Harrow" is also an idiom. To "harrow" a person is to distress them, to shake them up. To "harrow" a city or a region is to lay siege to it, to invade with an overwhelming force. Likewise, the Harrowing of Hell was said to be when Christ laid siege to hell itself, shaking its gates, terrifying its devils, and gleaning lost souls. I had a professor in seminary, Rev. Dr. Warren Smith, who likened it to a sneak attack on the devil's homeland, a rescue mission under the cover of the crucifixion. He called it "Christ's commando raid on Hell." Sounds exciting, right? So why don't we talk much about it anymore?

For those who, like myself, are in the Protestant world, the story doesn't seem to be that well supported by the Bible. The Harrowing of Hell is said to have taken place between Good Friday and Easter Sunday, after Jesus was crucified but before he was resurrected. Christ's soul supposedly descended into hell to bring at least some of those who were imprisoned there back with him to heaven. Yet none of the Gospel writers mention it.

The Roman Catholic and Eastern Orthodox Churches teach that there is some evidence for the Harrowing in the Bible. They say that Peter was talking about it when he said, "[Christ] went and made a proclamation to the spirits in prison, who in former times did not obey, when God waited patiently in the days of Noah, during the building of the ark" (1 Pet. 3:19–20). Others see this story in the book of Ephesians, where Paul quotes Psalm 68, asking, "When it says, 'He ascended,' what does it mean but that he had also descended into the lower parts of the earth?" (Eph. 4:7–9).

Modern biblical scholars don't seem convinced that Jesus literally going to hell was actually the point of either passage, but in more ancient times, the tradition of the Harrowing came to be a central theme of Easter and of the Christian story itself. It represented *Christus Victor*, the triumph of the cross, and God's deliverance from death. But the question remains, Why exactly would Jesus go to hell and who would he have brought back?

Even within traditions that take the Harrowing seriously, there are different opinions. Some believe that Jesus went to hell specifically to bring back the Hebrew patriarchs and the other heroes of the Old Testament, like Adam, Eve, Moses, and the prophets.[3] After all, if there was no salvation under the Law, and if faith in Christ is necessary to escape from hell, then Jesus must have gone down there to make a special trip to free all those holy people who died before he ever came on the scene. Who could imagine Abraham or Isaiah or any of the other Old Testament saints burning for all eternity because they happened to be on the wrong side of the cross?

Others say that Jesus went to hell to preach to everyone who had ever lived and died up to that time. He went in order to evangelize in hell just as he had on earth, giving all in hell the chance to come forward and believe, almost like some kind of infernal Billy Graham crusade. Of course, this leads to an obvious question: Under the pain and torment of hell, which they would all now know to be real, who would ever choose to stay? That's why some theologians said that Jesus must have gone down only to rescue those who lived holy lives while on earth, or at the very least only those who would have had faith in him had they been alive at the same time. This has become the dominant view of the Roman Catholic Church in the West.[4]

My favorite theory comes from the ancient Orthodox theologians of the East. In order to understand it, you have to get past the linear, calendar-based clock time we tend to think with here in the West. In the ancient East, Christians believed that time wouldn't work the same way in heaven and hell as it works on earth. We tend to think of eternity as an ever-clicking clock, a sequence of moments and days that simply extends on forever into the future. In the fourth and fifth centuries, theologians from the Alexandrian school of Christianity thought of heaven and hell as being an *atemporal* eon, or even a *transtemporal* age that runs not parallel with but adjacent to our own.[5] Under this view, our time here on earth occurs as an infinite series of moments, like a roll of film that never runs out, but heaven and hell exist as a single, resounding *now*, where everything and everyone exists at the exact same moment. For example, that's how Christ could theoretically appear in the furnace with Shadrach, Meshach, and Abednego, even though Jesus of Nazareth was not yet born. Once he ascended to the Father in Heaven, Jesus Christ left this single, forward-moving timeline and entered a state of pure timelessness, capable of touching all the cells of the film reel at the same time.

When this logic is applied to the Harrowing of Hell, it means that Christ went to hell not merely to preach to the patriarchs or the heroes of the Old Testament or even to rescue all the people who had lived good lives up to the date of the actual crucifixion. Rather, the belief is that Christ literally *destroyed* hell, and that he went to rescue every single person who ever lived or died in the past, present, or future. In this view, included in the throng of saved souls who were drug from the devil's grasp weren't just folks like Adam and Eve, Noah and righteous folks from the BC era. It also included everyone from all of history: you and me and our great-grandchildren and Hitler and Mr. Rogers. In a word, by descending into hell, Christ saved everyone.

You can see this theme clearly in Greek Orthodox Easter hymns of the period:

> "*Today* salvation has come into the world.... For having *destroyed* death by death, he has granted us victory and great mercy."

"You have led *us* out of Hell, Lord, by slaying the all-devouring monster, destroying his power by your might."

"From the belly of Hades has he delivered *us* and granted the *world* great mercy."

"When the Saviour went down as mortal to the prisoners, the *dead from every age* arose with Him. . . ."[6]

Notice that in these songs death is not merely defeated as in a battle, but it is *destroyed* with finality. These hymns testify that Christ's victory is not something that merely *happened,* but that it is something that *happens* now and *today.* And who does it happen for? It happens for *us,* for *the dead from every age,* and for the whole *world.*

As alien (or even heretical) as this all might sound to an average Methodist, Episcopalian, or Presbyterian, these themes of universal salvation and the destruction of hell pop up even in our own hymns from time to time, at least for those that have ears to hear them:

"When I tread the verge of Jordan, bid my anxious fears subside; *death of death* and *Hell's destruction,* land me safe on Canaan's side."[7]

"It was a strange and dreadful strife, when life and death contended. The victory remained with life, the reign of death is ended. So the scripture makes it plain, that *death by death's own sword is slain. Its sting is lost forever.*"[8]

"Mourning they laid you to rest, the author of life and creation; treading the pathway of death, *life now bestowing on all.*"[9]

So did any of this really happen? Did Jesus really burst down the gates of hell, free (at least some, if not all of) the people trapped there, and leave it a smoldering heap of rubble? I have no earthly idea. To be perfectly honest, when I think about it, sometimes I wonder if the whole story of the Harrowing of Hell is kind of like an ancient religious action movie . . . as if it was just a way of satisfying some deep need that Christians have to finally see a muscular, dominant Christ, instead of the humble, homeless carpenter who's always telling us to consider the lilies of the field and turn the other cheek. The descent into hell looks a lot more like a the kind of victory we're familiar with than does dying naked on a cross. In the Harrowing, we finally get to see a superhero Jesus who doesn't take anyone's shit, wrestles the devil into submission, and walks away while hell explodes into ruins behind him. That alone makes me doubt it.

On the other hand, I once read a sermon written by an old monk, St. Macarius the Great, one of those theologians from near Alexandria, that made me think differently. He compared the human heart to a kind of hell:

> "When you hear of sepulchres, do not think only of visible ones; your own heart is a sepulchre and a tomb. . . . Are you, yourself, not a Hell, a tomb, a sepulchre, a dead man toward God? . . . Well, then, the Lord comes into souls that seek after him, into the depths of the heart-Hell, and there he lays his command upon death, saying, 'Bring out the imprisoned souls that are seeking after me!'"[10]

Maybe the Harrowing of Hell is a myth, but like any good story, the true power of a myth is not that it *happened*, but that it *happens*. Why do I think Christ "harrowed" hell? Because he both *has done* and *is doing* it in my soul, and many others.

We have story after story of God laying waste to each and every hell we build for ourselves. The entire arc of the biblical narrative is about a God who refuses to abandon us to our own prisons, who comes down to dwell with us in the bad place, wherever it is

. . . under slavery in Egypt, in the furnace of pagan kings, or even on our own earth, at our own time, and in our own society, with all the angst, competition, and bloodshed that rules this world. It's about the Finder of the wandering lamb and the lost coin, the one who breaks down every door, opens every tomb we might build, and meets us wherever we are, whenever we are, only to offer us a hand, and say, "Let's go home."

the bureaucracy of the afterlife

Who are you to pass judgment on slaves of another? It is before their own lord that they stand or fall. And they will be upheld, for the Lord is able to make them stand.

—Romans 14:4

We Protestants just love our dichotomies. Whenever we can, we like to categorize anything and everything into tidy little binaries that help us make sense of the world: heaven and hell, wheat and tares, sheep and goats, saved and damned, you either accept Jesus or you don't. Everyone has their spot, and eternal destinies become a matter of simple classification. Did you have faith or not? Are you one of us or one of them? Will you go to A or B?

But when you think about it, the world isn't really like that, is it? We say that God created day and night almost as if they were intended to be these two separate compartments of time, yet dusk and dawn are in between the two, and they are arguably the two most magical times to be outside. Our maps show land and sea, yet we yearn to spend our precious vacation time at the beach, the ever-shifting boundary between the two. We tell our friends that we will be there for them "come rain or shine," yet we know well that most of life is lived in a kind of fog, a haze of good, bad, and indifferent. It's within these in-between, liminal spaces that we seem to find the most meaning, and it's here that most of us live most of our lives.

I wonder whether one of the reasons that Christianity is now struggling in cultures where it used to thrive has something to do with our inability to come to grips with a world that doesn't conform to the easy categories of A and B. Consider monotremes, like platypuses: venomous mammals that lay eggs and have flat bills and webbed feet that are reminiscent of a duck. Politics is quickly moving beyond the old liberal/conservative dogma favored by previous generations. Even human beings are not as easily categorized as we once thought they were, especially as we begin to reckon with the idea that gender and sexuality do not always conform to a specific binary. These things all exist on a spectrum, and, whether we are ready or not, the world is coming to grips with its spectrality. I happen to think it's high time that Christians do the same.

the wesleyan blueprint

I think that we want the afterlife to be a simple choice of A and B because that kind of dualism has always been the most politically expedient way of thinking about the world. When someone is running for election, designing an advertising campaign, or even trying to save souls, it helps to be able to paint the world in the starkest possible terms of black and white.

It's far too boring to explain all the excruciating minutiae of why you disagree with your opponent's policies or how your marginally different product might be better than the competitor's. It's much faster and more exciting to simply say that their product is trash and yours is genius or that their candidate is evil and yours is a hero. Likewise, it is quite burdensome and time consuming to sit down and speak to a friend about why they should change their life, explaining the spiritual benefits of being part of a church and having a relationship with God. It's much easier, more efficient, and more impactful to simply tell them that they are going to hell.

The exvangelical musician Derek Webb articulated the Christian desire for simple categories of black and white well when he sang,

> Don't teach me about politics and government
> Just tell me who to vote for . . .
> Don't teach me about moderation and liberty
> I prefer a shot of grape juice[1]

As a Methodist who has only ever used Welch's for Holy Communion, I feel a bit of a sting from that last line, but the message is clear enough: binaries are reductionistic, and, in most cases, they just don't work. Our choices are complicated, just like our lives. Faith and spirituality depend on context. Spiritual lives vary based on the people and the real-life situations in which they find themselves, and sometimes the right answer isn't always apparent.

Most of the people who sit in my pews were raised in the church, and of course there are some who convert later on in life. Those are the most common spiritual paths, and our theology accounts well for them. But what about those whose spiritual stories are different—like babies who die in childbirth? Or infants who pass away before they have the chance to be baptized or declare their faith in Christ? Are those who convert on their deathbeds to be treated the same as lifelong believers? Are there special rules for good people living in faraway lands who've never heard the name of Jesus? What about those who have such profound disabilities that it doesn't seem like they *can* declare their faith or even have faith at all?

I once knew a wonderful lifelong church lady who came to reject her faith while struggling with dementia. Did she really recant her religion at the end of her life, or was that simply the effect of a profound neurological disease?

There are plenty of pastors out there who just wave away such questions, mumbling something about grace and letting God sort it all out (something I've probably done myself)—but in many of these situations, that doesn't seem quite adequate. After all, these kinds of stories belong to real people. Some folks have borne children who never made it home from the hospital; some have friends who have been so hurt and abused by the church that they can't possibly pray to God without reliving their trauma. These stories need an outlet in the church. They need a place in our collective story. It's not enough to placate them with some kind of sentimental pleasantry and move on to more "normal" questions. So I ask again: what do we do with those folks who don't seem to fit neatly into box A or box B?

For many churches and congregations throughout history, answering that question involved moving beyond the A (heaven) and B (hell) paradigm and offering up a C, maybe a D, and even some Es and Fs. Some traditions imagine an afterlife that is full of different zones and compartments that can handle all manner of spiritual classifications. They try to solve the problem by expanding the binary into a larger, more complicated system, and, in so doing, they construct a kind of spiritual bureaucracy.

The founder of my own denomination, John Wesley, was notably prolific in this endeavor, especially for a Protestant. Although as an Anglican priest he denied the Roman Catholic doctrine of Purgatory as being "a thing vainly invented, repugnant to the Word of God," he tried his best to illustrate what the Bible actually had to say about the afterlife.[2] Being a very serious student of New Testament Greek, Wesley tried to organize a system that could account for each of those Greek words for heaven and hell in the New Testament that we talked about in the last chapter, and at the same time, he tried to answer some of those difficult questions about where people might end up after they die.[3] Wesley's version of the afterlife contained no fewer than six (!) different realms where souls might take up residence after death.[4]

First, he believed that a very small number of people go directly to heaven when they die. Wesley is distinct among Protestants because he believed that it was actually possible (though exceedingly rare) to reach a state of sinless perfection in this life. Those who could manage it would be deemed completely fit for God, and they would be immediately "glorified" and welcomed into an everlasting heaven.

However, Wesley thought that most souls would first enter into Hades (also known as Sheol, the Pit, or the underworld) when they die, which is itself split into two compartments: paradise (the good place) and Gehenna (the bad place). He believed that paradise was roughly equivalent to "bosom of Abraham" (Luke 16:19–31) and the place where the criminal on the cross to the right of Jesus went after he died (Luke 23:43). All saved people (including all babies and infants who die young as well as the righteous who've never heard of Jesus) go to paradise as they await the final judgment.

Likewise, those who are not saved and those who have recanted or backslid in their faith go to Gehenna, which for Wesley was a kind of hell-light. This is "the outer darkness" with "weeping and gnashing of teeth" (Matt. 8:12), but it isn't yet the final realm of everlasting torment. For that, we have to wait until the end of time, when Hades is emptied out and souls from both Gehenna and paradise are resurrected together to participate in the final judgment (an awkward meeting, if ever there was one). This final judgment is mostly for the sake of formality, however. Everyone from paradise will then be instantaneously perfected, glorified, and ushered into heaven, and everyone from Gehenna will be cast into hell-proper where they will suffer forever. Finally, at the center of hell is Tartarus, a place of extreme torment and suffering that has been set aside just for Satan and his fallen angels (along with Chronos and the other Titan gods, I presume). And that's Wesley on the afterlife.

If I could be frank for a moment: I hate this stuff. I am a committed United Methodist and the theology of John Wesley has been an inspiration to my life, but when he starts categorizing and organizing these kinds of supposed spiritual realities, I'm overcome with equal parts boredom and confusion. I recognize that Wesley at least takes seriously the nuanced language of the New Testament, yet I still have so many questions: What's the point of Hades and the final judgment? Why aren't those in paradise just immediately glorified and brought to heaven? And why aren't those in Gehenna just thrown immediately into hell? Why the waiting period? How long does that last? Can new evidence ever be introduced that could help their case?

Sometimes Wesley seems to miss the idea that the Bible is more *evocative* than it is *descriptive*. The Scriptures express deep truths about life and spirituality. They are steeped in poetry, narrative, and ancient symbols that are meant to humble us and make us think soberly about our lives and the effects we have on other people. Yet here, Wesley treats the Bible almost like some kind of atlas of the afterlife. Reading Wesley along with evangelicals and fundamentalists today, one is made to feel almost as if the Bible itself is poorly written—as if all the stories, symbols, and poetry are clues to some bigger puzzle below the surface that needs to be solved; as if underneath the Scriptures there is some grand theological system that we need to decipher, organize, and communicate.

If God wanted us to have a blueprint or a schematic of the afterlife, perhaps that's exactly what God would have given us. God could have made it clear, included a well-labeled map with a detailed legend, perhaps even an infographic, and left no room for interpretation or misunderstanding. Instead, we have all these words and concepts from ancient cultures that contradict, intersect, and interact with one another, presenting us with a rich yet utterly mysterious glimpse into what lies beyond ... and the best we can do is chop it all up and put labels on everything. Those labels don't really inspire. They give neither comfort to the grieving nor hope to the penitent. All these labels do is allow us to dwell in a false assurance that we're right, that we have it all figured out, and that we, better than anyone else, know how to properly categorize the world.

dante's dixie cup

Of course, Wesley couldn't hold a candle to the greatest afterlife bureaucrat of all time, Dante Alighieri. He speculated that hell had nine separate circles, Purgatory had seven levels and two antechambers, and heaven had ten Spheres of Ascension! Dante took the three compartments of the afterlife (heaven, hell, and purgatory) common to the European mind of the fourteenth century and blew them out, populating them with all kinds of characters, beasts, creative torments, and extravagant blessings. While his great work, *The Divine Comedy*, is not considered the official doctrine of any church or denomination, Dante has undoubtedly shaped the history of our understanding of the afterlife more than anyone else. Yet, when you read it closely, it seems he intended to shape history in a very different way.

In his first book, *Inferno* (or *Underworld*), Dante finds himself being led through hell by a Roman pagan named Virgil, the ancient Latin poet. It seems that Dante chose Virgil to be his guide in the underworld because Dante considered him to be among the most righteous and intelligent souls in hell. Virgil was most famous for writing the epic poem the *Aeneid*. This ancient story includes the great founding myth of the Roman Empire, the story of the brothers Romulus and Remus, who were raised by a wolf and who would come to found the greatest city in history. Through mythological genealogy and storytelling, the *Aeneid* makes the case that Caesar Augustus should be seen as the single, divinely ordained ruler of Rome and that under his leadership, Rome would come to rule the world. In other words, it was a kind of ancient propaganda.

At this point, it's important to note that Dante was a Floren-
tine and that his home city of Florence was considered a "daughter" to the ancient city of Rome.[5] In Dante's fourteenth century,
much of central Europe was supposedly united under the banner
of the Holy Roman Empire, led by an emperor who was considered to be the spiritual successor to Caesar, but it had neither
the unity, the wealth, nor the military might of Old Rome.[6] As
Voltaire is said to have quipped, "The Holy Roman Empire was in
no way holy, nor Roman, nor an empire." This new, pale facsimile
of an emperor was widely considered weak and ineffective, and
Dante was part of a political faction that wanted to strengthen
the emperor and elevate the empire. His activist party, the White
Guelphs, was frustrated with what they believed to be the pope's
interference in political life and saw him as an obstacle to the
rebirth of Roman glory. In an earlier book, *De Monarchia,* Dante
bewailed the sorry state of the current empire with its pathetic
emperor, and he called for a renaissance of the Roman Empire of
old, with a true and powerful emperor at its head.[7]

Is it any wonder, then, that Dante would be led by someone
like Virgil, a luminary of ancient Rome, to discover the mysteries of the afterlife? As Dante and Virgil make their way through
the nine circles of hell, they run into a fair number of politicians,
and wouldn't you know it—many of them were condemned to
hell because they were guilty of working against Dante's own
political ambitions![8]

When Dante gets to the lowest circle, Virgil tells him that
the very center of hell itself is reserved not just for Satan but for
all traitors, betrayers, and oath breakers. There, Dante finds the
ancient devil with three gruesome faces, each with its own horrifying mouth. The one in the center chomps eternally on the
greatest traitor of all time, Judas Iscariot, who is given the worst
punishment in all of hell for his betrayal of Christ. From a literary
perspective, this seems like an obvious choice. Of course Judas
would get the worst of it. He was, after all, supposed to be Jesus's

friend and disciple, and his betrayal, perhaps more than anything else, led to Jesus's crucifixion.

But it's the other two satanic snacks that are most revealing about Dante's true ambitions. Who, according to Dante, do you think were in the other two mouths? Pontius Pilate? King Herod? They were certainly among the greatest villains of the Bible. Perhaps he chose dastardly characters from the Hebrew Scriptures, like Nebuchadnezzar, Herod the Great, Jezebel, or even Cain?

Actually, in order to round out the trio in the center of hell, Dante didn't choose religious figures at all. Dante Alighieri, the political activist who was working hard to revive the glory and splendor of ancient Rome, imagined that the other two mouths of Satan eternally devoured Brutus and Cassius, two senators who betrayed and murdered their friend, Julius Caesar (the greatest Roman hero of all), before he could pronounce himself emperor.[9]

What's ironic about Dante's inclusion of these politicians is that in *De Monarchia*, he argued that the pope had too much political influence and that he should stay in his lane (so to speak) of religion and spirituality. But when describing a spiritual reality, Dante clearly had his own political axe to grind. Those who oppose the emperor, he seems to be saying, belong in the lowest circle of hell.

This is how spiritual bureaucracy works. We build systems and institutions and say that there are categories and regulations that everyone must fit and follow. We split the world up into good and evil, all in the name of God and the Bible, yet the very systems we create reflect our own biases and serve our own ends. How many native civilizations did Europeans conquer in the name of bringing religion to the "savages"? Do you think they did that to save souls out of the kindness of their hearts? Perhaps the incredibly profitable colonies and slave labor they gained were just a fringe benefit of such holy and selfless love of neighbor. (I hope you're picking up on my sarcasm.)

When I was a college student, I once went to the movies. I, being poor and having spent the last of my money on my ticket, didn't have the means to buy a costly soft drink at the counter, so I asked the lady for a free cup of water. She gave me an actual, grandma's-bathroom-style Dixie cup and told me to fill it in the drinking fountain. I asked her for a big cup, like they use for the soft drinks, but she just shook her head and said, "I'd have to charge you for a big cup. Rules are rules. Water goes in the little cups." I went over to the drinking fountain but discovered that some nihilistic terrorist had placed a wad of chewed gum on the button. So I came back to the counter and politely explained the situation. She explained once again that rules were rules, so I begged her, a kind and generous woman, to give me, a fellow child of God, a big cup of water.

As I filled my Dixie cup in the bathroom sink, I realized something: we like to think that our rules, policies, and laws all protect the common interest, that they are fair, just, and dispassionate. We imagine that when we split the world up into categories of right and wrong, legal and illegal, we do so out of deference to some objective sense of what's good and holy versus what is bad and damnable. That's what we *like* to think. But the truth is, often those rules and policies and institutions that we build, the ways that we categorize the world and the people in it, have more to do with nursing our own privileges and protecting our own interests than anything else.

The way we organize and categorize the afterlife is no different. Dante put Brutus and Cassius in the center of hell not because they had met some objective standard of evil that made them two of the worst sinners of all time but because it served his *own* political interests to do so. He may not have even realized it at the time, and he may have even had his own theological reasons for doing so. Nevertheless, when he imagined who the enemies of God might be, it turned out that God's enemies looked a whole lot like his own.

I don't think it's too far of a stretch to suggest that perhaps we do the same thing . . . all the time.

bent over with bureaucracy

The word *bureaucracy* literally means *the rule of the desks*. Bureaucrats are the ones who point to the papers on the desks of life and say, "These are the rules. This is the system. This is who goes where. Why? Because the desk said so." Christians often talk about the afterlife as if it's just a matter of bureaucracy: Did you have faith? Are you predestined? Did you carry out the sacraments? If yes, go here. If no, go there. If it's more complicated, then you may even end up here, or here, or here. Heaven, hell, Hades, paradise, Tartarus, Purgatory, limbo . . . It's all a matter of simply consulting the book on the desk. But figures like Dante remind us that the way we construct those categories, the manner by which we delineate and categorize and try our best to administrate eternity, says much more about us (our own values and priorities) than it does about God.

I don't know about you, but I'm much more interested in being judged by God than by a piece of paper on a desk that somebody claims to be God's "system."

I'm reminded of this lady from the Gospel of Luke (13:10–17). The text says that she was bent over for eighteen long years. Jesus heals her back and stands her up straight, but the leader of the local synagogue can only complain that Jesus healed someone on the Sabbath, breaking, in his eyes, the Law of Moses: "There are six days on which work ought to be done; come on those days and be cured and not on the Sabbath day" (Luke 10:14).

This was a religious bureaucrat if ever there was one. This spiritual gatekeeper took it upon himself to call Jesus out for not playing according to the rules, as if saying, "Jesus, who do you think you are? You can't just go around healing on the Sabbath! We have a policy. There's a system here!"

In an ancient Mediterranean world that was based on a culture of honor and shame, where nearly every public interaction was an opportunity to show up one's neighbors and glorify oneself, this particular rabbi took his chance to knock Jesus down a peg. Like Dante, the rabbi used a rule (or his *interpretation* of a rule) as an excuse to cover his own self-interest.

But the message of Jesus throughout the Gospels is that where bureaucracy fails, Jesus heals. Where bureaucracy dehumanizes and categorizes, Jesus calls us brothers and sisters and shows us the love of our Father. It seems to me that Jesus healing on the Sabbath, eating with sinners, making friends with tax collectors and prostitutes, and even forgiving the criminal hanging to the right of his cross serves to illustrate that the grace of God cannot be contained by the fragile rules and institutions we use to administer it. Where we give out paper cups, God's grace is a raging torrent of love and forgiveness that flows wherever it chooses.

the ultimate "dead" line

One of the most glaring bureaucratic policies that Christians like to promote is the rule that, for some reason, death is the ultimate cutoff for securing one's salvation. Most Christians simply assume that there is no opportunity for repentance or conversion after death and that something about dying irrevocably seals one's eternal destiny. Doesn't that seem a bit arbitrary? What is it about death that would keep the soul from accepting God's grace? Do the souls of the dead somehow lose the ability to repent for their sin? Why does there need to be a time limit, and how is that deadline fair if it is different for everyone?

Just a few verses after Jesus heals the bent-over woman, this exchange takes place:

> Someone asked him, "Lord, will only a few be saved?" He said to them, "Strive to enter through the narrow door, for many, I tell you, will try to enter and will not be able. Once the owner

of the house has got up and shut the door, and you begin to
stand outside and to knock at the door, saying, 'Lord, open to
us,' then in reply he will say to you, 'I do not know where you
come from.' Then you will begin to say, 'We ate and drank with
you, and you taught in our streets.' But he will say, 'I do not
know where you come from; go away from me, all you evildoers!' There will be weeping and gnashing of teeth when you see
Abraham and Isaac and Jacob and all the prophets in the kingdom of God, and you yourselves thrown out." (Luke 13:23–28)

It sounds to me as if someone asks this question to give Jesus the
opportunity to reaffirm the religious bureaucracy that he just at-
tacked by healing the woman on the Sabbath, almost as if they're
giving Jesus the chance to save face and reassure the crowd. It's as
if the questioner is saying, "Sure, you broke the policy by healing
a woman on the Sabbath, but surely you won't heal *everybody*,
right? Tell us that there is still some kind of system at work here.
Please confirm for us that only a select number will ultimately be
healed and saved after they die."

Jesus's response has all the hallmarks of a passage that's ripe
for a bureaucratic interpretation. He says they have to enter
through a "narrow door," hence the assumption that "only a few"
will be saved. He goes on to describe how there will be those who
knock and knock, only to be disavowed and thrown out to where
there is "weeping and gnashing of teeth." This passage certainly
makes it sound as if salvation is only for an elite few, that only
those who die with the proper credentials will be able to make
their way across the final velvet rope to the heavenly banquet, and
while everyone else will be turned away—but it only sounds like
that if you don't read it all the way to the end:

"Then people will come from east and west, from north and
south, and take their places at the banquet in the kingdom
of God. Indeed, some are last who will be first, and some are
first who will be last." (Luke 13:29–30)

Notice how this verse begins with the word "then." This is Jesus turning the tables of the conversation, saying that there is something that happens *after* the door is closed and some are turned away. Sure, the first part of Jesus's answer makes it sound as if some people will have the door slammed in their face, but "then," in the next verse, we see that this door is only closed temporarily, for people will come from far and wide, from all four directions and corners of the earth.

Let us be clear: this would have sounded like a form of universalism to first-century Jewish ears. To insinuate that God intended to save those who come from every people and nation would be something akin to heresy. It questions Israel's status as God's chosen people on earth, a key feature of Judean theology of that time.

To add insult to heresy, Jesus then tells them that "some who are last will be first, and some are first who will be last." Those who get there first and arrogantly knock on the door assuming that they will be the guests of honor (like a whole nation that thinks they are exclusively God's chosen people, or the disciples who are always arguing about which one of them is the greatest) will come to find out that they have to wait awhile (Matt. 18:1–4; Mark 9:33–36; Luke 9:46–47). Those who come late to the party will actually get priority seating while those who thought they were VIPs have to wait their turn. But if you read closely, you see that, at the end of the story, they still get in. By the time this lesson is over, the meaning becomes clear: a "narrow door" doesn't mean that most people get shut out. What it means is that there's a line, and some will have to wait a bit longer than others.

This is as close to a "system" of the afterlife as we are ever given in the New Testament. There are no compartments, categories, circles, or spheres. There is only a line with every kind of people from every kind of place making their way through the narrow, yet nevertheless very open, gate.

Over and over again, Jesus shows us the humanity of those we would put into different compartments from ourselves. He reminds us that our fellow brothers, sisters, and siblings are not so easily categorized and separated. To one another, we should not be enemies to be defeated, resources to be exploited, or infidels to be converted. We all belong to one another as one family, and we all belong to God as a heavenly Parent. So it only follows that we would all have a place through God's gate and at God's table, no matter how long it takes for us to get there.

heaven buddies

To illustrate this mutual belongingness, let's say there are two twins named Jack and Jill.[10] Imagine that they are just alike, that they were the very best of friends, and that they happened to be raised by a pair of particularly deplorable parents who taught them to be terrible people. They spend their twenties and thirties swindling the poor, burning down churches, and throwing eggs at chubby vicars—a damnable offense if ever there was one. Then, when the twins are forty years old, they're driving down a hill and get run off the road. Jack dies in the accident, and, being an unrepentant sinner, he goes to hell to be tortured forever. Jill, however, recovers from the accident, grieves her brother, and has a religious awakening. In a moment, the scales fall from her eyes; she gives her life to Christ, gets baptized, and then spends the rest of her days as a nurse at a leper colony. Upon her death some fifty years later, she's ushered into heaven, only to find out that her dear brother Jack has been suffering in hell all this time and that he will continue to suffer forever and ever.

Consider how Jill might feel at that moment, knowing that not only would she never see her brother again but that he would be endlessly tortured while she was *supposed* to be enjoying paradise. Yet in her heart, she knows that the only thing truly separating her from him was the arbitrary deadline of his early death. How would Jill enjoy heaven knowing that things could just as easily have been the other way around, had she been in Jack's seat and he in hers? Could heaven even *be* heaven for her? Wouldn't you expect her to beg God to just give her brother one more chance?

Some philosophers have imagined that heaven would be so wonderful that Jill's mind would be consumed with grace and beauty, and she wouldn't even spare a thought for her brother. Others have imagined that souls in heaven would rejoice in the sufferings of those in hell, knowing that the justice of their torment somehow brings glory to God.

To me, both of those ideas are barbaric. Are we really to believe that being glorified in heaven actually means being *less* compassionate (and, coincidentally, making us in our earthly state somehow more compassionate) than God?[11] Do those in heaven, those we refer to as "saved" and "redeemed," simply ignore those who they know to be suffering? Even worse, do they actually *revel* in the pain of those in hell?

If that's what it is for a soul to be saved, then God is not nearly as good as I was told.

Likewise, some would say that God might "touch the mind" of a glorified soul, blocking them from the pain of remembering loved ones who are accursed. But isn't that, as David Bentley Hart put it, comparable to some kind of "heavenly lobotomy,"[12] or at the very least, an eternal barbiturate?

For me, this is where the dark logic of heavenly bureaucracy finally breaks down. It seems to me that Jack's damnation would impede the possibility of Jill's salvation. For one to suffer for all eternity means that the other, too, would suffer, whether it be in heaven or in hell.

From the time of my childhood, I've had a number of painful orthopedic operations. I was born with a severely deformed right ankle that required several reconstructive operations and long periods of painful rehab. I hated these operations not just because they hurt me but even more so because I saw firsthand how my mother suffered by watching me suffer. The dramatic climax was when I was twenty-nine years old, and I decided with my doctor that it would be better to amputate than continue this never-ending cycle of surgical treatment. When the decision was made, I sat in my car and wept—not because I was about to go through the pain of losing my leg but because I knew my mother would *witness* me going through the pain of losing my leg. In that way, my mother and I are linked. My suffering leads to hers, and hers back to mine.

When I think about it, I can also imagine that I have this same kind of relationship with several people in my life: my wife, father, siblings, friends, and people from my church.

Allow me to submit that nearly all of us have at least one person with whom we are linked on this level, someone without whom heaven just would not be heaven—a heaven buddy, if you will. It may be a parent, a spouse, a child, or a friend, but most of us know someone whose damnation would mean our own, someone whom we love so much that we would suffer ourselves just knowing that they are suffering.

Might I then suggest that the more love we have for our neighbors, which is to say, the more Christlike we are, the more people will fill this role for us. The more loving we are, the more heaven buddies we have.

Could it be that the whole human race might just be linked in this way? I would suffer knowing that my heaven buddy suffers; that heaven buddy would have heaven buddies of their own, and they would suffer knowing that those people are suffering, and so on, until we see that the whole world is a network of compassion—throughout both space and time—that links our collective destinies together.

Finally, when we are "glorified" in heaven, when we are as Christlike as we will ever be, might it not also be the case that we will look on the whole world with Christlike compassion? Wouldn't we feel the same love, desire, and empathy for everyone that he does, regardless of whether we personally knew them?

If so, then it seems to me that we do not live in a world of categories, separate flocks of sheep and goats, wheat or tares, saved and damned, but rather, we live in a single, undivided web of heaven buddies. If one is damned, all are damned. And if one is to be saved, then all must be saved . . . eventually.

seven

the great work

I am confident of this, that the one who began a good
work in you will continue to complete it until the day
of Jesus Christ.

—Philippians 1:6

You can run on for a long time, run on for a long time.
You can run on for a long time, but sooner or later,
God'll cut you down.

—Johnny Cash,
"God's Gonna Cut You Down"

Whenever anyone starts to doubt the idea of a hell of endless torment, it seems there's always one passage that they
bump up against: the parable of the sheep and the goats from
Matthew 25:

All the nations will be gathered before him, and he will separate people one from another as a shepherd separates the
sheep from the goats, and he will put the sheep at his right
hand and the goats at the left. . . . Then they [those on his

left] also will answer, "Lord, when was it that we saw you
hungry or thirsty or a stranger or naked or sick or in prison
and did not take care of you?" Then he will answer them,
"Truly I tell you, just as you did not do it to one of the least
of these, you did not do it to me." And these will go away
into eternal punishment but the righteous into eternal life.
(Matt. 25:32–33, 44–46)

It says it all right there. Sheep and goats. Right and left. Eternal life
and eternal punishment. It's as clear as day, right?

I've heard plenty of sermons over the years that contrast the
nice, white, fluffy sheep who go to heaven with the dark, ugly
goats who go off to a hell of everlasting torment. Of course, this
kind of *dualistic* interpretation of who goes where in the next
world plays right into the hands of all those "isms" that are currently tearing this present world apart: racism, classism, national-
ism, ethnocentrism . . . But what choice do we have? This parable
is, after all, a story about division, about those who are accepted
and those who are rejected. As we walk around the world with
this story rattling around the back of our minds, assuming that
Jesus divvies us all up into good guys and bad, it is only natural
for us, in turn, to start categorizing the folks we see into sheep
and goats, people who are worthy of our love and attention and
those who deserve only our scorn and reproach. It seems that
the sheep and the goats are destined to be a lens by which most
Christians see the entire world: the lost and the saved, Republi-
cans and Democrats, gay and straight, . . . honest, hard-working,
Christian patriots and, well, everyone else.

(Tell me, when you just read the story of the sheep and the
goats, in which of those two groups did you imagine yourself and
your loved ones to be? Are you sure?)

As if that weren't bad enough, passages like this can leave us
with the sense that there are some people who are *essentially ir-*

redeemable. After all, a goat is a goat and a sheep is a sheep. That's just how they're born. It's not as if a goat can be somehow rehabilitated into a sheep. No amount of training or love can spin a goat's coarse fur into soft wool. It simply is what it is, and at least in this story, eventually every goat will get what's coming to it.

There are even those who follow a certain strain of Christianity (what some might call "double predestination" or "*hyper-Calvinism*") who believe these reprobate goats were, from the very moment of their conception in the mind of God, *intended* to go to hell. That's what God wants, and that's what God does. These lost souls, by virtue of their birth as goats, were always destined for torment. Their eternity is already fixed; there is nothing that they or anyone else can do to change it. The next step in this dark logic is that God literally created some people for the *purpose* of damning them and that, somehow, their everlasting torment in hell will bring glory to God.

I really hope that interpretation of this parable is as repugnant to you as it is to me. If that reading seems like a commonsense or even morally righteous approach to matters of the afterlife, then honestly, you should probably think about putting this book down now, because we have some very different ideas about who God is, and I'm afraid that the rest of this book might not do much to bridge that gap. But for the rest of us, what can we do? It's in the Bible, isn't it? What other interpretation is possible?

sheepyness

The first thing that's necessary is to take a step back and look at the spirit of the parable as a whole. If we become fixated on the categories of sheep and goats and the last few words alluding to some kind of afterlife, then we run the danger of overlooking the point of the passage itself. When we do that, it becomes apparent that the sheep and the goats are all part of the same herd belonging to the same Shepherd. I've heard this passage preached as though the goats are somehow intruders in the herd or that because they don't provide wool, they are somehow expendable. If anything, history seems to tell us that the opposite is true: most Judean shepherds were more likely to slaughter the sheep in order to eat their more tender and succulent meat and let the tough-fleshed goats stick around a little longer for the sake of their milk.

Also, notice that the sheep to the right of the shepherd are considered praiseworthy precisely because they do *not* think of the world in a dualistic way. They are sheep not because they were born as sheep but because they have chosen to respond to their neighbors in a very specific way. What grants them their identity as sheep is that they are precisely the kind of people who do not split the world up into sheep and goats. Look at the reason the Shepherd-King gives for praising the sheep on his right:

> I was hungry and you gave me food, I was thirsty and you gave me something to drink, I was a stranger and you welcomed me, I was naked and you gave me clothing, I was sick and you took care of me, I was in prison and you visited me. (Matt. 25:35–36)

The sheep respond to need and otherness with hospitality and love. They are sheep precisely because they are capable of recognizing a common humanity in their neighbors and having empathy for those who might be different from them or marginalized by society. They choose to cross the boundaries and break through the walls that might otherwise divide people— even the walls of a prison cell. Their "sheepyness" is defined by their refusal to accept the divisions of social or immigration status, health, wealth, or even (most ironically) the consequences of punitive justice.

Notice that the King does not say, "I was *innocent* and you came to prison to visit me." He does not seem to care about the particular guilt or the innocence of the one who is incarcerated. He simply identifies himself with whoever might be in prison, saying, "I was in prison and you visited me." As the last detail mentioned in a series, the fact that sheep go to visit prisoners carries the most emphasis in the text. Caring for those who are imprisoned actually *epitomizes* what it means to be a sheep. Yet, some will argue that we are to understand this passage to be saying that God imprisons souls in a torture dungeon and withdraws God's presence from them for all eternity! Are we to believe that God is praising the sheep for their enduring presence with those who are in prison, and at the same time, God withdraws God's own eternal presence from those whom God sends to prison? If that were true, then Christianity would simply be a terrible religion worthy of our rejection, because the Christian God would be the biggest hypocrite of all.

Remember that this story appears in the Gospel of Matthew, the same gospel where Jesus forbids retaliation against an evildoer and commands his disciples to love their enemies and pray for their persecutors (Matt. 5:38–47). And what is his rationale for making such ridiculous demands? "Be perfect, therefore, as your heavenly Father is perfect" (Matt. 5:48). In the Gospel of Matthew, time and time again, Jesus draws a direct line of correlation between the character of the Father and the character of his own disciples. Jesus defines the perfection of the Father by the love of enemies. The point Jesus makes here is that in loving precisely those who should elicit our vengeance, we actually imitate God the Father.

Being a Christian pacifist, I've had many debates about whether it is possible to kill someone and yet still love them. I don't believe it is, but I can at least entertain the argument. However, it is unfathomable to say that one can love someone while simultaneously torturing that person *for all eternity*.

In Matthew, the message of Christ is clear: disciples are to always attempt to do what God does, think as God thinks, and love as God loves. At its heart, the parable of the sheep and the goats simply can't be about splitting people into categories, creating divisions, or putting up walls at all, eternal or otherwise. It's actually about crossing divisions, transgressing the artificial walls and borders that separate us from one another, and finding a fundamental unity that is shared by all people and even Christ himself. "Sheepyness" is acquired through the imitation of the Shepherd-King.

the redemption of baby goats

So, then, what do we do with the last line? Why does the Shepherd-King divide out the goats and put them "away into eternal punishment" (Matt. 25:46)? How could this phrase be interpreted as anything other than a hell of never-ending torment?

I admit that in English, it can't. Those who only have access to this Scripture in the English tongue cannot possibly walk away from this passage without believing that there are "goats" who are destined for an eternity of torment. Unfortunately, this is one of those places where our typical English Bibles again struggle to capture the poetry and nuance of the biblical Greek (along with translations of the words *Gehenna*, *Hades*, and *Tartarus*).

For instance, even the English word "goats" is far too vague. In Greek, the word is *eriphoi*, and it specifically refers to kid goats, young and immature goats that were famous in the ancient world for being trouble makers. These rambunctious livestock were known to often wander off aimlessly or mingle among the sheep of the herd instead of staying where they were supposed to be.[1] The emphasis here is not the idea that the goats are somehow bad or irredeemable and that they need to be slaughtered or resigned to hell. It's that they are lost and immature and that they need to find their way back to where they belong.

But all that, of course, brings us to those two dreadful words . . . *eternal punishment*.

The original Greek term that corresponds to our word "eternal" is *aiōnios*. The difficult thing about the word *aiōnios* is that it represents a complex idea in ancient religion and cosmology, and we don't really have a single word that can tightly grasp its meaning.

If you read other Greek literature of the time, it becomes clear that *aiōnios* has never meant "eternal" as in "the forward advancement of time into infinity."[2] In its most literal sense, the word means "of the age" or "of the eon."[3] (We can still hear the shadows of this original meaning in some traditional Christian prayers that end with the line "unto the ages of ages. Amen.") There is another Greek word, *aidios*, that really does mean eternal as we think of it, but that is not the word that is used here or anyplace else in the New Testament where punishment in the afterlife is concerned.[4]

Aiōnios as an adjective means that something belongs to the next age, the eon after this one, the period of time after life on earth. It is "qualitative, not quantitative."[5] The word is not about duration at all.

To illustrate, let me take a crude example from the sad world of pop-Christianity: the so-called pearly gates. Some people (quite wrongly)[6] imagine that upon dying, everyone goes up to heaven and waits in a line where they have to be checked by Saint Peter at the pearly gates. Assuming that's true (it's not), it would make total sense to say that the line in front of the pearly gates is, in a manner of speaking, *aionian*, in that it belongs to the next age, that it has the quality of being on the other side of this life. However, it would be totally wrong to say that it is somehow "everlasting," which is what we mean when we say *eternal*. The line to the pearly gates belongs to the next world, the next age, the following eon, but that doesn't mean that it doesn't have an end. Theoretically, everyone will eventually get their turn in front of Saint Peter, and someday there won't be any people left in line. The line is finite. It has an end. In the same way, in Matthew 25:46, there's nothing about the word *aiōnios* that should make us think that the punishment is "eternal" in that it lasts forever. It's only eternal insofar as it belongs to the next age. In that sense, ironically, it might even be a more accurate translation to say "heavenly punishment."

One could say the very same thing about the "eternal fire" of Matthew 18:

> If your hand or your foot causes you to sin, cut it off and throw it away; it is better for you to enter life maimed or lame than to have two hands or two feet and to be thrown into the eternal fire. And if your eye causes you to sin, tear it out and throw it away; it is better for you to enter life with one eye than to have two eyes and to be thrown into the hell [Gehenna] of fire. (Matt. 18:8–9)

These flames are not eternal in the sense that they will last forever. They are aionian in the sense that they belong to the next eon. In the same way, the fire is unquenchable to us, on this side of the aionian divide, but they are not unquenchable by definition. I don't doubt that these flames are real (at least metaphorically speaking), that they are painful, or that they are a punishment of some kind, but surely we can all agree that an omnipotent God could quench them if that God so chose.

Worth mentioning here is Mark's version of the above teaching that ends a bit differently:

> And if your eye causes you to sin, tear it out; it is better for you to enter the kingdom of God with one eye than to have two eyes and to be thrown into hell [Gehenna], where their worm never dies and the fire is never quenched. For everyone will be salted with fire. Salt is good, but if salt has lost its saltiness, how can you season it? Have salt in yourselves, and be at peace with one another. (Mark 9:47–50)

Here the fires of Gehenna are referred to as "salt," which in the ancient world was known for its ability to preserve and purify.[7] After warning us to take care that we are not cast into the aionian fire, Jesus seems to say, among other things, that (1) such fire is actually, somehow good; (2) everyone will inevitably be "salted" with it at some point; and (3) the effect of this "salting" in the present is peace among the disciples. In this way, the aionian fires of Gehenna seem similar to the refiner's fire of Malachi 3 or the pool of fire and brimstone in Revelation 20 and elsewhere. They all seem to refer to a temporary trial of discipline that is meant to cleanse and purify rather than torture or destroy. While the effect of such fire might be pain, its ultimate purpose seems to be the education and the sanctification of all those who might receive it.

an eon of pruning

In order to explain what I think the word *punishment* means in the New Testament, I first have to tell you about my little trees.

As I write this, it's currently autumn here in Ohio. Fall is my favorite season for, among other reasons, it means that it's bonsai trimming season. For those who may not know, bonsai is a kind of horticultural art form that comes from East Asian countries. The word *bonsai* is Japanese, and it literally means "tree in a pot." The goal of bonsai is to grow beautiful, healthy trees that take on all the proportions of fully grown trees in nature, yet are still small enough to fit into pots and be placed on benches for display.

Bonsai is a treacherous hobby to begin. There are about a hundred ways to kill a bonsai tree. For one, trees obviously don't like to grow in pots with their roots constricted. They require an expensive, well-draining soil from Japan, special fertilizer applied at very precise times throughout the year, and near-constant attention. Trees have to be watered daily, rotated for optimal sun exposure, and checked for bugs; most importantly, limbs and roots must be pruned very carefully for the sake of both health and beauty. Prune too little and the roots get bound and limbs die off. Prune too much and the tree cannot survive.

All of this puts a strain on the health of these little trees. Every time you cut a branch or pluck a leaf, you injure the tree. Every time you take the tree out of its pot to trim the roots and give it new soil, the tree gets shocked. Even the pot itself is a crucible for a tree. Inside the pot, it can't spread out its roots to find nutrients. It can't send a taproot deep into the ground to find water. It isn't permitted to grow in just any way it chooses. It's almost as if the tree has to learn how to accept the care of the gardener, how to embrace the pot and the frequent pruning, and how to trust that it will get the water and the fertilizer it needs. In a Christian manner of speaking, the tree has to figure out how to rely on the grace of the one who watches over it.

Some trees struggle. Others don't make it. But those that do become some of the most gloriously beautiful and long-living plants on the face of the earth. In your garden at home, a juniper can expect to live maybe eighty to ninety years, given favorable conditions and few changes in the landscape. But in a pot, with the constant care and attention of generations of dutiful gardeners, a juniper can live hundreds of years, perhaps even longer. One of the oldest known junipers is a bonsai kept in Shunkaen, Japan, and it is over eight hundred years old. The oldest bonsai is said to be a ficus tree kept in Italy that is over one thousand years old. In the National Bonsai Museum in Washington, DC, there's a white pine bonsai that's over four hundred years old. What makes that particular tree special is not just its age but that it survived the blast and subsequent radiation of the Hiroshima atomic bomb.

Given the right nurture, pruning, and love, the lifespan of any bonsai tree is indefinite—perhaps even perpetual.

I've found that caring for bonsai is a very spiritual experience, as is all gardening (which is probably why it's a very consistent metaphor in the Bible). It feels as if I develop a kind of relationship with all my trees. Seeing them grow and thrive warms my heart, and seeing them struggle or wilt makes me feel guilty. When pruning time comes around, I get excited initially. Then, when the tree is actually in front of me and the scissors are in my hand, I experience a kind of holy dread. I am reminded that what is cut cannot be uncut. I am sobered by the thought that even though I'm about to make the tree more beautiful and hopefully help it thrive in a way that it would not be able to do on its own, I'm about to hurt the tree, about to damage it, to make it, for lack of a better word, sick. Hopefully, the harm that I inflict upon the tree with my own fallible hands will not be a "sickness . . . unto death" but rather "for the glory of God" (John 11:4 KJV).

This dread reminds me that even though mine is the hand that punishes, it does so only out of a certain responsibility: to help and not to harm. This, I imagine, is similar to the responsibility that ought to guide parents in disciplining their children, teachers in educating their students, and doctors in performing surgery. In each case, the parent, teacher, or doctor may need to inflict a kind of punishment from time to time upon those who are entrusted to their care, but we trust that they will perform this solemn duty with only the best interests at heart for the one being punished.

An exception to this might be what we expect from our judges. In the American justice system, "punishment" is a murky term. When someone calls for another person to be punished by a judge or magistrate, it isn't always clear what purpose they would have that punishment serve. It seems to me that most people conceive of judicial punishment in one of three ways: restitution (the paying of a fine or a reparation in an attempt to make amends for a wrong committed), retribution (a painful penalty that deters future misdeeds and offers catharsis to the victims of a crime), and rehabilitation (the upbuilding of a criminal's character). Which of those do you think Americans think of most often? Which of those do you think is closest to what Jesus had in mind when he spoke of punishment?

It's not easy to understand how our sin could be simply "paid back" to God in the form of restitution, and if it could, we are assured over and over again that such a payment has already been made on our behalf by Jesus's atonement on the cross (Mark 10:45; 1 Tim. 2:6; 1 Cor. 6:20, etc.).

Likewise, if you bracket everything we were taught about hell and simply consider the words of Jesus and the apostles, doesn't the concept of retribution sound decidedly *unchristian*? To think that our pain could somehow be cathartic to God, that it would bring God some kind of pleasure or relief to see God's own children tortured, seems like the worst form of blasphemy.

The only kind of punishment that makes sense for God, considering everything that Jesus Christ came to teach us about the Father, is punishment for the sake of growth, for beauty, and for rehabilitation.

Every time I read the word "punishment" in the New Testament, rather than a fiery cave of a prison, filled with dark souls screaming in torment, I actually think of my bonsai trees. *Kolasis*, the Greek word for "punishment," is primarily a horticultural term used in gardening, orchard keeping, and vine dressing. The most fundamental translation of the word is "pruning," and it was only used by way of analogy to represent the punishment of a person. Just as a tree or a vine must be pruned in order to produce fruit more efficiently, so a person must suffer a kind of pruning for the sake of their own fruit. The precise meaning of "pruning" might differ from one context to the next. In a family, a child might be grounded or even spanked; some sort of prison sentence might be handed down in a judicial setting; extra homework might be assigned for a struggling student, and so forth. But in each case the purpose is (hopefully) the same: redemption.

Kolasis is the kind of punishment that is performed for the sake of development and reform. Rather than restitution or retribution (which is a totally separate word in Greek), it's intended to be remedial or even therapeutic. Clement, a fourth-century bishop of Alexandria, Egypt, a native Greek speaker, made the distinction clear:

God does not punish [*timoreitai*] ... since punishment is the
retribution of evil with further evil—, but corrects [*kolazei*]
for the sake of those who are corrected.[8]

In English, the word *punishment* might be a technically correct
translation, but it's so vague that it is almost purposefully mislead-
ing. *Kolasis* is a specific kind of punishment, one that is carried out
with a precise purpose in mind: the benefit of the one being punished. A better translation would be "discipline" or "chastisement."
When Jesus speaks of the goats going away to *kolasin aiōnion*,
rather than "eternal punishment," we should instead translate it
as something like "the eon of pruning," or as David Bentley Hart
masterfully renders it, "the chastening of the age."[9]

until . . .

I do not object to the idea that God punishes us. If God is indeed
a Father (or Mother or Parent of any kind), it would only make
sense that God would discipline God's children with growth and
redemption in mind. It would be immoral to imagine God *not* doing that. What I find both morally repugnant and without warrant
in the New Testament is the idea that such punishment would be
eternal and without the hope of redemption, rehabilitation, or,
most importantly, forgiveness.

For instance, Jesus gives us the parable of the unforgiving servant in Matthew 18. There we meet a servant who is forgiven a debt
of ten thousand talents of silver. The "talent" is a unit of measure-
ment that, in the New Testament period, equaled approximately
59 kilograms or nearly 130 pounds. That means the servant was
forgiven a debt of 650 tons of silver. In the story, the servant then
demands payment from a fellow servant who owes him a measly
one hundred denarii. At the time, such a sum would be worth
about three hundred dollars. Of course, when the king hears about
this, he is outraged, and Jesus tells us, "his lord handed him over

to be tortured until he would pay his entire debt. So my heavenly Father will also do to every one of you, if you do not forgive your brother or sister from your heart" (Matt. 18:34–35).

Certainly, this story is a stern warning about the danger of not forgiving as we have been forgiven. It beautifully contrasts the immensity of the grace that God has shown to us with the pettiness with which we often treat one another. Yet most of the sermons I've heard on this parable eventually focus on the word "torture" and use it as just another instance of Jesus warning us to steer clear of the never-ending torments of hell. But that interpretation fails to notice one key word: "until."

The debt that the servant owes may be mind-bogglingly humungous, but the parable itself still assumes that there will come a time when the debt can be paid. It's hard to imagine how being handed over to torturers could possibly pay a debt, and it's even more unimaginable to consider how long it would take to pay back a debt equaling 650 tons of silver, but nevertheless, the very inclusion of the word "until" means that however long it may take, it cannot be forever.

There are similarly apocalyptic themes in Matthew 5:26 and Luke 12:59, where Jesus warns against being thrown into prison "until you have paid the very last penny." Again, the word "until" makes all the difference. He could have just as easily made it clear that the debt would never be repaid, that we could never be released, that the pain would continue forever and ever, with no hope of relief. Yet the text does not say that. The "until" reminds us that however long the sentence we serve, however great the debt, however hot the flames, or however long the age of our pruning, there will come a day when the One who began a great work in each of us will indeed bring it to completion.

eight

protestant purgatory

Hell, Purgatory, and Heaven seem to differ the same as despair, fear, and assurance of salvation.

—Martin Luther, Ninety-five Theses, thesis 16

G rowing up in a United Methodist congregation, I was never taught the differences between our particular Protestant denomination and any other. I never knew what separated Methodists from Presbyterians or Baptists or nondenominational folks until I studied religion in college. As far as my family and friends were concerned, we were all just sort of *generically* Christian. Even today, when new folks who are "church shopping" come to visit my own church, I can tell that they are looking more for "feel" than anything else. On the whole, people care much more about things like worship style, preaching quality, and overall friendliness than they do about the distinctive theological traits of denominational traditions.

However, one distinction most people still make is between Protestants and Catholics.[1] To most Protestants, Catholicism feels like a completely different thing. When I was young, it seemed strange and distant, almost like a foreign culture or a different religion altogether. Participating in church youth group and even studying at a religious school, it was not unusual at all for me to hear someone refer to the distinction between our traditions not as between "Catholic and Protestant" but between "Catholic and *Christian*," and it was always expected that we would remain the latter.

I can still remember my youth pastor's warning about the three *p*'s of Catholicism: pope, priests (meaning confession), and the worst of all, purgatory. The idea that Catholics would believe in a pope whose words would be considered infallible or that a person might be expected to confess her sins to an intermediary priest who would declare forgiveness on behalf of God was bad enough,[2] but to believe that there might some kind of a *third* place in the afterlife, a place between heaven and hell . . . that was utterly beyond the pale.

For those who may not know, the word *purgatory* literally means "purification." It is the name that the Roman Catholic Church gives to the idea that even "for those who die in God's grace and friendship," there is a final purification that is needed "to achieve the holiness necessary to enter the joy of Heaven."[3] It's important to note that in Catholic thought, purgatory doesn't exist between heaven and hell so much as it does between earth and heaven. While one's personal salvation within the church guarantees one's right to heaven, there are a whole host of smaller sins and mistakes one might still need to deal with before one can be "cleared" for eternal life. This means that even for the "saved," there must still be some "purifying fire" that cleanses the soul and makes it fit for the presence of God.[4] In this way, purgatory isn't so much about punishing sins as it is about healing or cleansing the effects of sin on the soul, preparing it to spend an eternity with God.

Think of the prophet Isaiah, who is beckoned up into the very throne room of God only to cry out, "Woe is me! I am lost, for I am a man of unclean lips, and I live among a people of unclean lips, yet my eyes have seen the King, the Lord of hosts!" (Isa. 6:5). As holy as the prophet may have been, to behold the glorious presence of God was utterly incompatible with the sin that yet dwelled within him. In this state, the presence of God couldn't be enjoyed or even tolerated. It could only be feared and lamented. Fortunately, a seraph angel picked a flaming coal from the altar, flew over to Isaiah, and held it to his mouth, saying, "Now that this has touched your lips, your guilt has departed and your sin is blotted out" (Isa. 6:7).[5]

The Catholic doctrine of purgatory is the idea that we all need our own piece of coal. By the time we die, most of us are not pure enough to be ushered directly into the presence of God (those who are completely pure upon their death are called, in Catholicism, "saints"). Purgatory is the name given to the means by which those sins are burned away.

As of late, the Catholic Church seems less comfortable referring to purgatory as a *place*, like heaven or hell. It's more common these days to hear Catholics speak of purgatory as more of a mystical process, with Pope Benedict XVI even seeming to suggest that the cleansing fires of purgatory are, in fact, an encounter with Jesus after death: "Some recent theologians are of the opinion that the fire which both burns and saves is *Christ himself*, the Judge and Saviour. . . . This encounter with him, as it burns us, transforms and frees us, allowing us to become truly ourselves."[6]

It's common to find people (even some Catholic worshipers) who misunderstand the doctrine of purgatory, thinking that the church is saying that there is some kind of a middle ground between salvation and damnation, a place where souls simply languish in a dull nothingness, caught forever in a gray limbo between heaven and hell. But that's not it at all. Purgatory is temporary and reformative. It's not an alternative to salvation; it is part of the salvation process itself. Catholics would say that every soul who enters purgatory is destined to leave it and join their God in heaven.

Of course, this is all completely unacceptable to Protestants. After all (at least according to my youth pastor), Protestants only believe in the *Bible*, right? And certainly purgatory is *not* in the Bible!

Except that Roman Catholics would insist that in the Bible you can find purgatory all over the place.

They might point to Revelation 21, which speaks of the heavenly city at the end of time, saying, "nothing unclean will enter it" (Rev. 21:27). As with the prophet Isaiah, the very presence of God demands purity. It only makes sense that even one who is saved might need to be purged of a few venial (incidental) sins before entering the eternal city.

Likewise, Paul seems to offer prayers on behalf of a dead man, Onesiphorus, in 2 Timothy, asking that he would receive "mercy from the Lord on that day" (2 Tim. 1:15–18). What need would such a man have for Paul's prayers? Why pray for the dead except to help them as they undergo something potentially hurtful in the afterlife? Why would they need mercy if all is already accomplished? It must have been, so the reasoning goes, that Paul understood that Onesiphorus was still on his way to full salvation, and as he prayed for him in life, Paul found it to be appropriate to pray for him in death as well.

In the deuterocanonical book of 2 Maccabees, Judas Maccabeus orders that sacrifices be made in the temple for any Judean soldiers who may have died while wearing pagan amulets for good luck (2 Macc. 12:38–45). Again, it seems that these warriors for God were mostly ready for heaven, having given their lives for God's chosen nation, but they perhaps still needed a little help after death to get rid of a few incidental sins that might have otherwise kept them from experiencing the full joy of their salvation. Maccabeus orders that the sacrifices be made in order to hasten their journey in the afterlife.

Finally, Roman Catholics would draw our attention to many of the Scriptures we mentioned in the previous chapter that seem to speak of a refining fire, debts that are to be repaid while someone remains in prison, and forgiveness that takes place after one dies. In the Catholic imagination, these are references not to hell but to something mysterious that happens to the saved soul after death. They describe a spiritual process by which the soul is prepared and purified for everlasting life.

only through

As I mentioned earlier, my leg was amputated in 2012. Before that time, the pain from my ankle was so constant and intense that an amputation was the only rational option to save my quality of life. After the surgery, I went straight from the hospital to an orthopedic rehab facility for three weeks to gain strength and mobility for the difficult time between the amputation and when I would receive my first prosthesis. Those first few days of physical therapy were really hard. My residual limb was swollen to the size of a bowling ball, and it ached and throbbed like nothing I had ever felt before. Just allowing my leg to dangle off the side of the bed was almost too excruciating to bear. Because of earlier surgeries, I was already adept at walking on crutches, but doing so with a half-severed limb swinging below my torso was nearly impossible.

My physical therapist had a mantra she would repeat over and over again every time she saw that I was struggling and it seemed as if I wanted to give up. Whenever I had to grit my teeth in pain or tears started welling up in my eyes, she calmly but decisively reminded me, "There's no way out but through. There's no way out but through."

Don't get me wrong—that amputation was a good thing. It allowed me to stop using painkillers every day, and with my prosthesis my mobility has never been better. The amputation was absolutely necessary. I even count it as a blessing, but struggling there in rehab, with all that pain and frustration, it felt as if I was being punished. Through the amputation I had already received my salvation, so to speak. A better future had already been sealed into my life, but I still had to work through the painful healing that was necessary to prepare me to receive that salvation in all its fullness.

This is the underlying logic that Catholics see at work in the Bible. Christ has forgiven and saved the souls of the faithful, but their sin must still be dealt with through healing, maturity, and growth, which most often entails something like rehab: a mixture of discipline, time, and sometimes pain. It's not enough to assume that God would simply wave God's hand over those who die in the embrace of the church, instantaneously cleansing and sanctifying them and getting rid of every bit of impurity they carried with them into the afterlife. If God would do that ... if God *could* do that ... why wouldn't God have done it to everyone already? Why wait until after we die? Why not simply do it to all those who are still living, thus helping us rid our earthly lives of the suffering our sin causes?

Because such a move on God's part would not be true *redemption*. It wouldn't be the transformation and restoration of the image of God that we are promised throughout the Bible. It would be, in fact, something more akin to magic.[7] The Bible shows us time and time again that even though God forgives us of our sins, God does not simply make them disappear. The sin must be really and truly conquered through the blessed combination of divine grace and human will. It must be dealt with. That's what theologians call the *economy of grace*. That's just how it works. There is no way out of sin except through the process of sanctification.

Ironically, I think I can appreciate the Catholic doctrine of purgatory because of my Methodist roots. John and Charles Wesley, the founders of our tradition, believed very strongly that God's grace isn't merely a forgiving grace or a pardoning grace, as wonderful as those things might be. They also believed that it's a *transforming* grace. Methodists believe that God doesn't turn a blind eye to the wounds of our character. God gives us the time and the (sometimes painful) therapy we need in order for our wounds to actually heal. In the Methodist economy of grace, the soul must be rehabilitated.

Too often, Protestants imagine that salvation is no more than forgiveness, that God simply forgets about our sin as if all that's necessary is that a line be drawn through a number on some heavenly ledger. In Methodism and other Holiness traditions (like Wesleyans, Nazarenes, and some Pentecostals), salvation is more than that. God recreates us, making us both whole and holy. Such traditions believe this happens only through the formation of character, the purging of those habits and defense mechanisms that turn us away from love. This kind of spiritual formation entails both time and discipline—and often pain.

Of course, the Wesleys believed that the entirety of this process can only take place before death, in *this* eon, while the Roman Catholic Church teaches that this process can continue past death. While the word *purgatory* itself is found nowhere in the Bible, nevertheless the Catholic Church finds purgatory in the spiritual world the Bible describes. For Catholics, it is a natural and organic conclusion that grows out from the economy of grace and transformation shown to us throughout the Scriptures.

I agree with them.

As a matter of fact, I agree with them so much that I see no reason to limit the healing process and effects of purgatory to those who die as professed Christians, or to anyone else for that matter. It seems to me that it is much more biblical (and much more in keeping with Jesus's revelation of the character of God) to believe that everyone, regardless of their faith commitments here on earth, will also have access to that same burning coal. Everyone will have their sins pruned and amputated after death. Everyone will experience the refinement of those same purifying and *therapeutic* fires that Roman Catholic doctrine insists are set aside only for the faithful members of the church.

My point is simply this: *Hell is, for lack of a better word, purgatory.* I believe that everything the Catholic Church teaches about the process and purpose of purgatory is actually what we've been calling *hell* all these years.

hell as purgatory

Allow me to explain. As with purgatory, we know that hell isn't really in the Bible either (chapter 3). As I've already discussed, the word *hell* doesn't occur anywhere in the original languages of the Scriptures, and where we do find it in our English translations, we know that it's nothing more than a sloppy and biased replacement for complex theological and poetic concepts like Sheol, Gehenna, Tartarus, and Hades (some of which were borrowed whole cloth from other religions).

We also know that the idea that the Bible speaks of *everlasting* punishment is also flawed. As I have shown, the Greek word that we translate as "eternal" (*aiōnios*) is actually an adjective that describes something as belonging to the next age or eon, and there's nothing about that word that would have made its original readers think that it meant such punishment would be endless.

And finally, we know that when the Bible does speak of aionian punishment, it must be talking about a kind of punishment that always leads to the growth and the development of the one being punished. The Greek word *kolasis*, which we often translate as *punishment*, is much better understood as "chastisement" or "pruning." When the New Testament speaks of God's punishing God's children in the afterlife, it is always speaking about a process of healing discipline, burning away the dross of their lives and helping them grow into the Image and Likeness in which they were originally created.

This is similar to the process that Catholicism seeks to articulate when it talks about purgatory—the often slow and even painful application of divine therapy to a human soul for the purpose of healing it and making it fit for the eternal presence of God. It is, in fact, the *exact* same process—the only difference being that

Catholicism insists that there is a limit to the sanctifying power of purgatorial fire and that God's healing grace can be extended only to those who work out their desire for God before the arbitrary date of their death.

I, on the other hand, believe that some form of purgatory is waiting for everyone. Sam Wells put it best when he described this purgatorial version of hell in a sermon:

> For the Mother Teresa and the Francis of Assisi, we can imagine there's very little burnt off, and the refiner's fire is pretty much a painless process. They have accepted the forgiveness of God and been transformed by the sanctification of the Holy Spirit. They're pretty much in the clear and in Heaven they'll be instantly recognizable. But the Adolf Hitler and the Joseph Stalin are another matter. Almost everything in them, so we imagine, turned away from the grace and transforming love of God in Christ, and forgiveness was something they never sought. But here's the twist . . . we cannot simply say they are evil without giving up on the all-pervasive grace of God. So what we say is that for people like them the refiner's fire is an agonizing and almost total experience, and what's left [at the end], is pretty much unrecognizable.[8]

Wells is describing an afterlife that falls on a spectrum rather than in two different compartments. It is not enough to talk in terms of heaven and hell or the sheep and the goats. Just as infections, cancers, and other diseases occur differently and with varying levels of severity in every patient, so we all bring different levels of spiritual illness with us into the afterlife. Just as every patient entering a hospital is treated with fully customized care and therapy that is suited just for them and their particular body, every soul that crosses over the grave will receive the exact amount of grace it needs, regardless of how painful its rehabilitation may be.

We might imagine that some souls need nothing more than the spiritual equivalent of a couple Advil and a tall glass of water, while others need something like a full course of radiation and chemotherapy. Such ailments of the heart could be so severe that treatment could take years, generations, or perhaps even millennia. Nevertheless, the life and character of Jesus Christ reveals that our Physician is willing, qualified, and guaranteed to bring about the full health and recovery of every single patient.

a million plastic statues

To Protestants, this idea of a purgatorial hell can be shocking and offensive for two reasons. The first, as we have already covered, is that there seems to be something in us that actually *wants* there to be a hell of endless torment (chapter 4). While I've come across some good-hearted people who only *begrudgingly* believe in everlasting torment because they think the Bible requires it, there are plenty of others who actually seem to be *pleased* with the idea that some people will suffer forever and are unwilling to consider any possible alternative. To these folks, it just feels right and just that some would be punished to the greatest extent imaginable, whether they're thinking about people like Hitler and Stalin, their own abusers, or just "those people" who are out there in the world somewhere doing dastardly things.

I must admit that there is something of this attitude inside of me. I can think of people who have hurt me, people who have hurt my friends and my family, people who have been hurting people all over the world, and there is some part of me that would take a certain satisfaction knowing that they were spending eternity in perpetual torment. Some dark corner of my soul actually wants them to pay, to suffer, to feel the searing heat of unending divine wrath. It feels good to imagine that fate for them. It feels righteous, as if my own life has been vindicated and someone else has been forever labeled as the "evil" one.

Yet, when I'm at my best moments—at prayer and doing my best to remain "clothed with Christ" (Gal. 3:27)—I realize that desire is disordered. I should want true justice to be served and acknowledge that their sin (like my own) has a price. But their sin is not infinite. Their debt is not eternal. Their illness is not unto death. The day can and will come when they will be free, clear, and healthy, and I need to work on developing that hope within myself.

Put differently, I believe that God is strong enough to save even the worst among us, including those of us who actually want to see some people suffer forever and ever.

God is strong enough to save the Hitlers of the world, the child rapists, the animal abusers, and all those whom I deem unworthy of salvation—and God is strong enough to heal that part of me that is scandalized by such profligate mercy.

There's a particular politician (who, that I might avoid Dante's mistake of politicizing the afterlife, shall go unnamed) whom I absolutely despise. When I think about this person, I can find no goodness in him whatsoever. He seems perpetually angry and ungrateful. His mind seems utterly scattered except when it is obsessed with his own greatness. Everything he says and does seems offensive to me and at odds with everything I believe. It's not too much to say that part of me *hates* him, even though I've never met the man. I cannot imagine him deserving any less than complete and total damnation.

So I bought a statue. I keep it in my office (since my wife won't let me keep it in the house). It's a cheap plastic sculpture of the politician, except that instead of his usual angry scowl and power suit, he is sitting cross-legged with his eyes closed, apparently meditating while he wears the robes of a monk. I think someone created and sold it as a joke, but there is a look of peace and serenity on his face that reminds me both of his potential and of his ultimate fate. The statue softens my heart for him and for all those whom I consider to be my enemies. Sometimes I look at it and imagine what it might be like to sit with him, after he's been through his refining fire and I've been through mine, reclining in our final blessed peace together as we appreciate the God who saved us both.

In my mind I try to make a little plastic statue like that for every grudge I keep. I try not to imagine my enemies according to my own perception, but instead I work on beholding them with the eyes of God. I look for the person they will become when all the dross is burned away, all the potential is fulfilled, and all the wounds and sicknesses are healed. I don't always do such a good job, but sometimes, if only for a moment, the veil is lifted, and I can almost catch a fleeting glimpse of the ultimate salvation that is waiting for them. I hope they are straining the eyes of their souls to find the same in me.

stephanie's room

The second thing that can offend us, especially Protestants, about purgatory is that we would prefer to think of death as being an end. After someone dies, we like to comfort ourselves with the idea that they are now finally looking down at us from a "better place." If they have been battling a long illness or a slowly worsening cognitive disease, we like to imagine that their struggle and discomfort is finally over, that they are "resting in peace." To imagine that there is still work to be done and pain to be had violates the very sentimentalities that we use to console one another in times of grief.

As I wrote this very chapter, I was saddened by the death of one of my mentors in the faith, a deeply spiritual woman named Stephanie who helped set the course of my life in ministry. She had struggled with cancer for some time, continuing to work diligently as a pastor. While she was alive, it grieved me that she didn't yet have the means to retire from her work and enjoy the respite of her golden years. Since I was writing this book as I heard the news, I immediately thought about how badly I wanted to affirm both to her family and to myself that she was at rest and free of her pain. Yet, given everything I've written, I felt like I couldn't say that for sure.

But then I remembered what Pope Benedict said above, that perhaps the fires of purgatory *are* Christ himself. He invites us to think of purgatory not as an obstacle to be overcome in order to receive access to Christ but instead as a space where we can receive the unmediated companionship of our divine Teacher and Friend.

How many of us long for time away with a spouse or a friend or our children so we can remove ourselves from the demands of work and home and focus entirely on those relationships? By the same token, how often has our discipleship been distracted by the minutiae of earthly life? How often have we yearned for the time and space to devote ourselves wholly to the task of spiritual growth through building our relationship with God yet been prevented because things always seem to get in the way and we have too much to do?

Stephanie took many retreats over the years precisely to get away from such distractions. Having that uninterrupted time with her God was important to her. It was a value that she held close and gave to those around her. I even remember how she took her own money to build a prayer room in her little church, a special place set aside for the sole task of inviting folks to get away from the busyness of their lives and look Jesus straight in the eye. It had candles, a kneeler, and a lounge chair. She put a rug on the floor. Bibles, pillows, and prayer books were strewn about. The faint smell of incense always hung in the air, and there was a Christ candle right in the center of it all.

Sometimes I would swing by the church at odd times, and I would hear her praying and singing hymns by herself in that little room. I would see the tendrils of incense spilling out from the cracks in the door, and I knew not to bother her. She was in there enjoying time with her Jesus.

I smile now, imagining that Stephanie's purgatory might be like the ultimate version of that prayer room: a place far away from the cares and worries of this life, where she can sing, pray, grow, transform, and just be with her Jesus, face to face, without anything else to get in the way. Except this time, the flame at the center won't represent Christ; the flame will *be* Christ.

For someone like Stephanie, that kind of purgatory would be a rest. It would be a blessing and a relief to be freed from all the entanglements of life so she could bask in the transforming presence of her Lord. For someone like me, perhaps less so. That flame may feel a bit hotter and I might have to spend a bit more time there than I might otherwise prefer. But it will still be good, and a better place than this earth because I'll finally get the chance to focus on building the relationship with God that I've too often neglected on this side of the grave.

Likewise, for the selfish and greedy politician I mentioned above, I imagine that when he first starts out, it'll be a bit warmer and less comfortable still. Oh, who am I kidding? I think it's probably gonna be pretty damn hot in there, and I think he might rage and curse and be there for quite a while.

But then the day will come when all three of us will grow out of that little room because we won't need it anymore. We'll be clean and rested and ready for what comes next. The pain and struggle of the past will be but a memory and, clad with our white robes, the three of us will all meet around the heavenly banquet table to feast on God's love together.

And no one will be too late.

nine

the circles we draw

God is an infinite sphere, whose center is everywhere and whose circumference is nowhere.

—Hermes Trismegistus,
Book of the Twenty-Four Philosophers

Will the circle be unbroken, by and by, Lord, by and by?

—Ada B. Habershon

In Latin, *universus* literally means something like "a single rotation" or "a full turning." Picture someone standing in a circle, pointing their camera in a given direction, and then turning all the way around, 360 degrees. They've pointed to all of it, all the way around the compass. Their vision is, therefore, "all-encompassing." They've captured everything there is for them to see. They've made the circle whole. Their sight is, as we say, universal.

Of course, that circle does not go on forever. There is a limit to human vision, even aided by photography. There is also a limit to the very real social and cultural circles that we draw around us. In some ways, a lot of what we study as history can be read as our attempt to find, see, and understand the circles we think that we belong within. Whether we are talking about families or clans or tribes or nations or empires, there is a sense in which we long to be *circumscribed*, to know what our universe is, even as we consider our circle in the midst of the greater circle—the one true *universus*.

We like to draw these circles geographically, using borders and boundary lines, but we also do it ethnically, religiously, culturally, and historically. These days, with the advent of our communication technology and social media, we've taken to drawing our circles digitally, around common interests and something we've come to call "identities," things like sexual orientation, gender, race, and a whole host of other things that may or may not have anything to do with those who are in our immediate vicinity.

Nowadays, our circles need not have anything to do with physical proximity but are, rather, something we've internalized. We carry them with us. While we can no doubt be a part of more than one at a time, and while these various circles can intersect and have overlapping interests, we still defend our membership within them and seek to delineate just who can and cannot rightly claim membership in our circle. A lot of blood and ink has been spilled throughout the centuries defending and defining our circles.

There is a tender moment that happens deep in the sixth chapter of the Gospel of John that makes me think of the circles we draw. In the first half of the chapter, we see Jesus performing miracles. He feeds the five thousand, walks on water during a storm, and mysteriously seems to transport himself across the Sea of Galilee so that he can be alone. When the crowds, spellbound by his deeds of power (especially the making of all that food), chase him down, he launches into a long discourse about how the bread they truly seek is, oddly, his flesh. The Judean authorities challenge him, and he responds as plainly as he can: "I am the bread of life. Your ancestors ate the manna in the wilderness, and they died. This is the bread that comes down from heaven, so that one may eat of it and not die. I am the living bread that came down from heaven. Whoever eats of this bread will live forever, and the bread that I will give for the life of the world is my flesh" (John 6:48–51).

Then the camera turns to the large group of disciples following Jesus. When they heard what he said to the Judeans, they lamented to one another, "This is a hard teaching. Who can accept it?" (John 6:60, translation mine).

There's something about the struggle and the humility of that statement that gets me every time. The disciples admit that they either don't understand or don't even *want* to understand just what it is that Jesus is trying to say to them. There's an honesty there that most of us would struggle to match today.

The disciples get a bad rap for being dense and for misunderstanding the things that Jesus was trying to tell them. Personally, I take comfort in knowing that these folks followed Jesus around for as long as three years, saw the miracles with their own eyes, shared bread with him around a fire night after night, and *still* didn't get it. We look back at them from the perspective of some two thousand years of doctrine and theologizing, and we scoff at their ignorance. But they were digesting (pardon the pun) this stuff in real time, trying to connect the dots while it was all unfolding right in front of their eyes. It makes me feel better when I realize that there is so much I still haven't understood, so many ideas with which I have not yet reconciled myself.

When I've preached on this passage before, I've usually assumed that the disciples were scandalized by Jesus's sharp, almost cannibalistic rhetoric. Eating flesh and drinking blood? That kind of language would offend anyone. I assumed the disciples were also upset by the thought that all this eating of his flesh might somehow entail his death, an idea they are loath to accept elsewhere (e.g., Mark 8:31–33; 9:30–32; 10:32–34). The idea that his death would somehow be a victory just didn't make any sense to them at the time.

I think about the passage differently now. Yes, the language around eating flesh and drinking blood is odd, gruesome, and scandalous, but these days I wonder if it wasn't another word that had them so upset: *whoever.* "*Whoever* eats of this bread will live forever" (John 6:51, emphasis mine).

If Jesus had said, "Any Judean who eats of this bread will live forever," no one would have batted an eye. "Anyone who keeps the law" would have been more palatable to the disciples and the Pharisees alike. "Any child of Abraham" would have been even better still. The entire history of ancient Israel was based on the idea that salvation belonged to their specific nation, the sons and daughters of Abraham who were brought through the Red Sea and across the Jordan into the promised land. The locus of salvation fell around the nation of Israel, the holy *ethnos*.[1]

By using the word "whoever," Jesus expands the borders of who's in and who's out, scrambling their notions of who gets to receive the grace of God and how they get to receive it. By opening eternal life to "whoever eats of this bread," Jesus begins to deconstruct that old bureaucratic system of circles and opens up eternal life to ... well ... whoever! It isn't about blood or lineage or culture or tradition. It has nothing at all to do with any of the circles the people of God had previously drawn. Perhaps the disciples were scandalized because they wondered, "Could it be just *anybody* who eats the bread?" Maybe they even worried, "Could it be ... *everybody?*"

Exclusion is easy. Walking around thinking that we are the special ones, that we are justified simply by virtue of who we are or what we believe, some identity or another, is comforting. Cutting more and more people out of that circle isn't a problem as long we stay nestled safely inside of it.

Expanding the circle, however, is a "hard teaching." Expand it too far and we start to wonder if there's anything special about us at all.

By that measure, universalism might just be the hardest teaching because it expands the circle all the way.

interrogating our circles

We shouldn't be surprised that universalism is as scandalous as it is. After all, when we say that God's love knows no boundaries, we are describing something that is totally alien to our experience. Our love *does* know boundaries. We can't even imagine what it would be to love without boundaries. We have only so much strength, so much energy, so much time, so much patience, and so forth. We protect our circles of love because to expand them too far would risk exhausting all our resources. We have to limit the people we love, the issues we care about, and the values we hold sacred because we simply wouldn't be able to survive any other way. We have to draw our circles carefully because, in a sense, they contain something of our selves.

Whenever we're expected to express our care to someone new, there's a gut check that happens, a kind of calculation that occurs without us even knowing it. Do I have the resources for this? Can I handle one more person or cause to care about? Will this take something away from me and from the others who are under my circle of care?

That's why being a pastor is a perilous job. You're always pushing people to expand their circle and potentially deplete their resources further and further. I try to remind myself that it's not just that people don't want to expand, it's that they don't think they can. When they want to "circle the wagons" and exclude others based on this or that ideology or identity, it's usually because they're afraid of being drained, of not having anything left over for those who are closest to the center of their circle. In a way, that's a condition that's worthy of sympathy.

However, there are two mistakes we can make here. The first is to imagine that the people who are outside of our circle don't deserve our love, care, or attention, whether it's because of something they've done, someplace they're from, or just who they are. The second is to imagine that they don't deserve *God's* love, or that they are outside of God's circle, for those same reasons.

It's one thing to admit that I cannot actively love this or that person or be passionate about this or that cause due to my own limitations and finitude. It is quite another to profess that God cannot, and it's even worse to say that God *should not*. There's nothing wrong with admitting that we are limited in our ability to love. There is something wrong with using our limitations to justify exclusion and hatred in the name of God.

So put yourself in the shoes of the disciples for a moment. What happens in your gut when you hear the word "universalism"? What kind of images does the word conjure in your mind? What are the objections that spring up in your heart when I tell you that God loves and saves everyone? Who is it that you imagine cannot possibly be in God's circle? What are the rationalizations that lead you to think that God doesn't have the resources for a full "turning"?

progressive pluralism

Sometimes when I tell people that I'm a universalist, it becomes obvious that what they think I mean is that I'm a pluralist. A lot of folks seem to imagine a group of universalists to be like a drum circle of hippies lounging around a campfire, trading puffs and pontifications that all religions are, like, just different parts of the same elephant, man.

Oddly enough, I've known some liberal and progressive Christians who actually seem to be attracted to this image. They think universalism means the abolition of all circles (rather than the presence of one, all-encompassing Circle), the final end of the distinctions that have caused so much pain and division in the past, and the truth that religion itself is culturally arbitrary and ultimately doesn't matter.

This is the same reason why conservatives hate the idea. They see universalism as the ultimate infiltration of "liberal wokesters" trying to infect the Christian economy of grace with a kind of theological Marxism. The goal of it, they imagine, is a world where forgiveness is redistributed and everyone gets treated the same regardless of how truly undeserving they might be. By making grace available to everyone, the thinking goes, universalism would carry on the socialist project of removing the qualitative differences between people, abolishing hierarchies, and rendering all value judgments meaningless. To their minds, this would render salvation itself worthless, because as we all know, scarcity is what makes something valuable.[2]

So to liberals and conservatives alike, let me be clear: When I say "universalism," I am not referring to a kind of vain religious pluralism that says that all human religions are somehow equally true and equally valid and equally good. Don't get me wrong: in the realm of secular politics, a kind of pluralism is good and necessary for protecting fairness and equality from a public-policy perspective. But in the realm of theological discourse, both within and among the world's religions, pluralism can be ultimately self-defeating. Extreme pluralists like to think that they are promoting diversity and the recognition of beauty in every religious tradition, but in order to do so, they inadvertently erase a lot of what makes some of those religions beautiful in the first place.

I know someone who is a self-described pluralist. He's not the kind of person to ever consider questioning anyone's religious belief or hold any tradition as being somehow "more valid" than any other. On any given day, he might be quoting Saint Francis, leaving his crystals out to get charged up in the light of the full moon, consulting his horoscope, practicing tantric yoga, reciting Sufi poetry, or praying to an ancient pagan deity.

As a preacher and as a friend, it seems to me that the problem is that he never fully *inhabits* any of the traditions from which he is constantly improvising his own personal religion. (We've had many conversations about this.) By constantly skimming across the practices of each faith depending on what suits his mood on any particular day, he robs himself of the ability to plumb the depths of wisdom that any one of those traditions has to offer. Thus he is left hopping from the surface of one spiritual practice to the next, using various and disparate rituals, prayers, and proverbs as short-term prescriptions for his perceived existential ailments without ever taking the full course and sticking with any one of them long enough to treat the chronic conditions of his heart.

When I was a kid, I used to love going to the local buffet. I was enamored by the diversity of choice, seeing all that food laid out before me: salad, buffalo wings, fried rice, pizza, roast beef—what could be better?

It wasn't until I was older and first sat down for a seven-course meal at a traditional French restaurant that I learned cuisine, much like religion, can have a depth to it that one could never find at a smorgasbord. The whole meal took over three hours, and there was no buffet or salad bar, not even a menu! I didn't get to choose what food was put before me. I had to trust the chef, her years of training, the training of those who trained her, and those who trained the trainers, going back hundreds of years.

There's just something about investing the time and patience to savor each bite and letting a curated meal unfold before you that makes a truly unforgettable dining experience. While you might not like every single thing on your plate, it nevertheless makes you realize that there are some flavors and experiences you would have never chosen for yourself. Although it might not have filled me up the same way as other restaurants, putting myself at the mercy of a trained chef was somehow more satisfying than a buffet could ever be.

Part of what makes religion so powerful is that it contains lessons and wisdom from the past that I would have never scooped onto my own plate. Because I have given myself so fully to a single tradition, as ultimately right or wrong as it may turn out to be, I get to experience the richness and nuance of two thousand years of wisdom rather than the insipid tastelessness of a New

Age religious cafeteria, where I am offered lots of choice but little flavor and no true depth.

There are some religions, like Buddhism, Hinduism, and Baha'i, that are pluralist by definition, and those religions are, even from what little I've gleaned from my own pitiful research, full of wisdom and indescribably beautiful. They rightly recognize that no one religion has totally cornered the market on wisdom, yet none of them could be said to be *fully* pluralist. Even they still have some ideas about what constitutes a *good* expression of religion.

For instance, there are some Christian churches that have openly supported the assassination of doctors who perform abortions. There have been small, factional Mormon congregations that practiced plural marriage into the twenty-first century and arranged marriages between children and adults. We've all seen news reports about radical Islamists who actively subjugate women. Ancient Babylonian worshipers sacrificed their children to Moloch.

These religions are obviously not somehow all equally true or good. Even if we were to bracket the question of how conflicting accounts of the true nature of the universe can somehow all be true at the same time, we still have to consider the cultural expression and the moral consequences of faith. Religions seek to form us into certain kinds of people. Just as trees are judged by their fruit, we have to acknowledge that there must be such a thing as a bad religion, and even the most progressively minded among us ought not be scared to say so. While I may live in a pluralistic society where we have good rules about discrimination, I have to be true to my conscience, which tells me that there are religions that can lift the soul and transform the heart and others that can do unspeakable harm. It seems foolish to deny that fact, and possibly arrogant.

But it would be equally arrogant to proclaim that just because someone is caught in a life-wilting, society-harming religion, they are somehow doomed for all eternity.

grabbing the elephant

About five hundred years before the birth of Christ, somewhere on the Indian subcontinent, a now-familiar story started to circulate about blind men all touching a single elephant. As the story goes, one of the blind men was grasping the trunk and remarked that surely an elephant is like a python. Another wrapped his arms around a leg and said that the elephant must be like a tree. Another reached the ear and argued that, no, an elephant is more like a fan, and so on. The point is that because each man has only a limited perspective, he can only describe the part of the elephant that he can touch, and each one foolishly imagines his part to be the whole.

A version of this proverb can be found in nearly every major Indian religion today, including Hinduism, Buddhism, and Jainism, and it has been popularized in the West by the Baha'i faith and Unitarian Universalism, both of which often use it as a metaphor to describe each of the world's religions as a kind of blind man grasping only a part of the elephant of ultimate reality yet insolently assuming that it has comprehended the whole.

There is wisdom in this story. Surely none of the world's religions ought to claim that they have some sort of supreme and complete grasp of the metaphysical world. Insofar as the story of the blind men and the elephant inspires humility, dialogue, and tolerance, it's a great story, but even for all its modesty, it still contains a trap.

Consider the narrator, the one who supposedly witnesses the scene unfold and relates the folly of the blind men. The narrator only recognizes the foolishness of the blind men because she believes that she sees the elephant as it really is. She puts herself outside and above the perspective of the blind men and dares to tell us how reality really works. She takes the position of some kind of objective observer who sees the whole tableau, never admitting or realizing that she also feels only one part of the elephant, or that there is some unseen truth to which she has no access. Is that not the greater arrogance?

In other words, the drum circle of folks proclaiming the end of all circles is still, in fact, a circle all its own, is it not?

When pluralism is applied in secular spaces like legal cases, educational institutions, and political matters, it's a great tool that can help us see past our differences and unite around shared goals and aspirations. In that context, pluralism can keep us humble and open to one another. It can keep us from oppressing one another. In a manner of speaking, it keeps our circles soft so that when we bump into one another, we don't do more damage than we should.

In fact, I would say that because of Christianity's history of colonialism and oppression, because of the damage Christians have done to other faiths and cultures, we now have a particular responsibility to promote and safeguard pluralist public spaces. Our faith has spent so many centuries silencing other faiths that it is only right that we do whatever we can to make sure they have opportunities to make their voices heard.

However, when pluralism becomes a religion all its own, when it is promoted not as a cultural tool but as an overarching ideology, an ultimate truth above all truths, it can lead to cultural arrogance and erasure. Why study the depth of the world's religions if they are all ultimately the same thing anyway? Why devote oneself to an ancient tradition and way of being in the world if, ultimately, any one religion is only defined by the ignorance of its own perspective? Why seek truth at all if all the seekers of the past were actually, in their own way, just blind?

I'm not here to say that religion doesn't matter. I'm not here to erase cultures and identities and the wisdom of centuries that have something to teach every one of us. Thus, I would never say that all religions are the same or that the religion one chooses doesn't ultimately matter. I can hardly imagine a *less* progressive thing to say.

Quite the contrary. Religious differences testify to the beauty of humanity and are, I think, part of the splendor of creation itself. I contribute to that splendor best when I articulate *my* religion as it has been handed down to me, even as I acknowledge the limited perspective of my faith. I believe that when that tradition is properly understood and interpreted, it teaches that Christ is "the way and the truth and the life" (John 14:6) and that "through him God was pleased to reconcile to himself *all things*, whether on earth or in heaven, by making peace through the blood of his cross" (Col. 1:20, emphasis mine). That reconciliation is, in the most robust form of the word, *universal*. It is *all-encompassing*.

I believe that, ultimately, everyone is saved by Christ, both in this life and in the "aionian" life to come. Is the spiritual tradition by which I came to that conclusion flawed? Absolutely. We have blind spots that we don't even know that we have. Yet, it is not the tradition that saves; it is the Christ who inspired the tradition. Whether that Christ has been revealed through the Vedas of Hinduism, the Eightfold Path, the Talmud, or the Qur'an, I cannot say for certain. I can only say that the revelation that I have received through my tradition speaks of a God whose love is so expansive and so extravagant that somehow it catches the whole of the universe up in its mercy. Therefore, the universalism I am arguing for is, necessarily, a Christian universalism.

Notice a key difference. I'm not saying that everyone *must* become a Christian. I'm not arguing for the supremacy of my circle over the others, as if the goal should be some sort of Christian hegemony that somehow "wins" by either conquering or evangelizing the world. The universality of the gospel has nothing to do with the expansion of my circle or with the erasure of all other circles. I'm saying that my tradition teaches that around all of our good and beautiful and weird and even bad circles there exists an even larger one, one that encompasses us all.

The circles to which I myself belong are numerous: white, American, cisgender, straight, United Methodist, Christian. I try to acknowledge that all those circles are there, whether for good or for ill. I try to keep them as soft and pliable as I can, and I try to build relationships outside of those circles, but they exist nevertheless.

But I also believe that there is a larger circle by which all those circles, and in fact all possible circles, are ultimately circumscribed. Circles labeled "believer" and "unbeliever" both fit neatly under its curves. "Those who do good" and "those who do unspeakable evil" are not so far apart that they, too, are not bound by its mighty and loving ring. For the Christian universalist, that great circle of Trismegistus whose "center is everywhere and whose circumference is nowhere" is called "Christ." It is his circle that encompasses all our circles, even the one we might label "human," and, perhaps, even more than that.

more than a word

My all-time favorite word in any language is undoubtedly "apokatastasis." This Greek word literally translates to "back to the beginning" but is most artfully rendered as "restoration" or "resolution."

The word did not start out as a theological term; it was used first by ancient Greek medical doctors to refer to a return of health to the body, by ancient diplomats to speak of a hostage restored to their home country, and by ancient astrologers to describe a heavenly body that, having made a complete revolution in the heavens, found its way back to the same position in the sky.[3]

Apokatastasis took on a new theological dimension when the Hebrew Scriptures were translated into Greek. There, it's used to describe God returning Job back to his "rightful place" after he suffers at the hands of Satan (Job 8:6). While Ezekiel acknowledges that Sodom and Gomorrah got what was coming to them, nevertheless, he says, they will be returned "to their former state" (Ezek. 16:53–55). The very last sentence of the prophet Malachi speaks of the return of the prophet Elijah: "He will turn [or "restore," "resolve," the verb form of *apokatastasis*] the hearts of parents to their children and the hearts of children to their parents, so that I will not come and strike the land with a curse" (Mal. 4:5–6).

Perhaps you can see a theme here. *Apokatastasis* isn't just about putting something back where it was; it's about putting something back where it's *supposed* to be. It's not just a return to a previous state but a return to a *rightful* state, the state that it was supposed to have been in all along. In that sense, *apokatastasis* is about a rescue, a reconstitution, a putting *right* of what once went wrong.

This theme comes through loud and clear in the New Testament. On four separate occasions the Gospel writers use *apokatastasis* to describe the moment when Jesus heals someone, restoring them to health (Matt. 12:13; Mark 3:5; 8:25; Luke 6:10), which is simple enough.[4] But then in Acts, Peter gives a sermon at Solomon's Portico in the temple, and he uses the term in a much more apocalyptic sense: "Therefore repent, and turn to God so that your sins may be forgiven, so that times of revitalization may come from the presence of the Lord, and that he may send the Messiah chosen for you, that is, Jesus, who must remain in the heaven until the time of the restoration [*apokatastasis*] of all, which God announced long ago through his holy prophets" (Acts 3:19–22, translation mine).

Here is where *apokatastasis* turns from a simple word into a *doctrine*, a teaching worth believing in. It does not refer to the restoration of Israel, the restoration of a single soul, or even the restoration of all *people*; rather, it is simply the restoration of "all."

"All what?" you may be asking yourself. All believers? All good people? All the members of my particular denomination who have my particular beliefs?

I would answer simply that when Peter (and Paul, as we discussed above in chapter 5) says "all," he simply means "all." Everything restored, everything set right, everything put back into the place for which it was originally intended.

As a pastor, I particularly like to offer this verse to those in my congregation who are mourning the loss of a pet. In the past, the Christian faith has not offered much hope for pets or wild animals or anything that is not, strictly speaking, "rational." That's because somewhere along the way, we've forgotten about *apokatastasis*. We've forgotten that the restoration of our hearts is but a prelude to a larger, grander restoration—the universal restoration, a "new heaven and a new earth," as John put it, "coming down out of heaven from God, prepared as a bride adorned for her husband" (Rev. 21:1–2).

I've actually seen people cry when they hear that even their dear departed dog is part of God's circle. I had a neighbor who wept when men came to cut down a dying tree that she had planted in her back yard some forty-odd years prior, before her children were even born. She hugged me when I told her about *apokatastasis*. She was absolutely overjoyed at the idea of a tree being redeemed! How much more might God care about us?

If Satan really does have a three-headed dog named Cerberus, I wonder how he would react if you told him that his pooch would one day be redeemed as well. I wonder further how he would react if you looked Satan himself in the eye and said, "And so will you."

After all, if *apokatastasis* is about the redemption of all things to their rightful place, if it's about putting right what once went wrong, then wouldn't even the devil have to be redeemed eventually?

sympathy for the devil

I know this will strike some as controversial, and others might even consider it heresy, but I believe . . .

. . . that *Return of the Jedi* is the best *Star Wars* movie ever made. (Spoilers ahead!)

I saw the original trilogy when I was twelve years old and I got the special box VHS set for Christmas. Even before that, I knew all about heroes like Luke Skywalker and Princess Leia, and of course I knew that Darth Vader was one of the baddest villains of all time. I watched the first two movies in one day, and then the next morning, I was so angry at the events of *The Empire Strikes Back* that I couldn't wait to see Darth Vader's imminent demise at his son's own hand (pun intended, for those in the know).

I wasn't ready for what happened next. In the climactic battle, Darth Vader actually saves his son's life, and it becomes clear to the audience that he has, in fact, turned from the dark side toward the light!

The very idea that Darth Vader would be *redeemed* in the final act . . . I had just never seen anything like that before. Every story I had ever heard up to that point involved the bad guys being *defeated* but not truly restored. I was used to seeing bad guys getting killed, being banished to some other dimension, or simply going to prison. To my knowledge, I had never seen a film or read a story where the bad guy is really and truly *reformed* by the final moments. The point was that no matter what, the bad guy always had to be punished, and they always stayed angry and resentful right to the bitter end.

And then I watched *Return of the Jedi*, and the final scene featured the ultimate villain as a healthy, glowing force ghost (the *Star Wars* version of eternal life) smiling at his son alongside his long-lost friends. Darth Vader had heaven buddies! I was shocked, but I was also satisfied by it in a way that I had never been before. Somehow, the redemption of Darth Vader was a more *complete* ending than merely the death or defeat of Darth Vader would have ever been.

In that same way, in the grand narrative of creation that God is writing, wouldn't the mere death and destruction of Satan and his demons be less satisfying than their redemption? Wouldn't it signal to us that God is somehow too weak to offer us a more compelling ending? Wouldn't it mean that God is not strong enough, not patient enough, and not *attractive* enough to woo demons back to the fold?

Allow me to put it differently: Does God *hate* Satan and his demons? I'm no demonologist, but it seems to me that if one believes that devils are real, actual beings, then it stands to reason that God created them just as God created you and me. So have they somehow turned the God who *is* love, as 1 John 4:16 says, against them?

If you only read our English translations of the Bible, it would certainly appear so. Near the end of Revelation, there is a scene that appears to describe the moment when God has finally had enough and ultimately defeats Satan and his demons: "And the devil who had deceived them was thrown into the lake of fire and sulfur, where the beast and the false prophet were, and they will be tormented day and night forever and ever" (Rev. 20:10).

Well, that pretty much settles it, right?

Absolutely not. Remember from chapter 5, the "lake of fire and sulfur" is not merely a burning lake but a *pool* of fire and smelting chemicals. It is a metallurgical place, a place of cleansing and refining.

To be fair, the Greek word that is usually translated as "tormented," *basanizō,* is used elsewhere as a synonym for torture or torment, as one might do to extract information from an enemy, but even that is a kind of linguistic analogy. The most fundamental meaning of the word is, again, metallurgical. It is the word for testing a substance against a touchstone to see whether it is gold. A much better translation in this context would be "tested" or "tried."

And of course, in its original Greek, it does not, in fact, say "forever and ever." As we covered in chapter 7, the Greek word here is *aiōnios,* which does not mean "eternal" but "age."

So put together, the passage should read, "And the devil who deceived them was thrown into the smelting pool of fire and sulphur, where the beast and the false prophet were, and they will be tried and tested, day and night, for ages of ages."

An age is a long time, but it is not forever. "Ages of ages" would be a *really* long time, but it is not forever and ever.

It is disingenuous on the part of our Bible scholars and translators to suggest that this passage and those like it represent the final destiny of Satan and his demons. On the other hand, it would also be disingenuous for me to say that the Bible explicitly describes their salvation. All any of us can say for certain is that God is love and that the devils will be tried, tested, and purified for a very long time. You can do with that what you will.

But if you ask me, I'll say that all things being equal, eternal damnation is just a really bad story. A cold heart that stays cold. A clenched fist frozen in angst. A circle that stays broken forever. An incomplete victory. What could be more boring than that?

ten

kicking and screaming

Thou hast formed us for Thyself, and our hearts are
restless till they find rest in Thee.

—St. Augustine of Hippo, *Confessions*

People only mention that it's a free country when
they're doing something shitty.

—Demetri Martin

There's a funny argument that's pretty common in the theological circles of evangelical Christianity. It's that, essentially,
a hell of eternal torment is necessary if humans are to have freedom. For salvation to mean anything at all, so the logic goes, there
must also be damnation. If we are to truly love God, then we must
also be free to perhaps reject God, and if we are given the option
to love God for all eternity, then we must also be free to reject
God for all eternity. Hell, then, is nothing that God does *to* us,
but rather, it is a choice that we make for ourselves and that we
(apparently) keep making for all eternity.

This was the view represented by C. S. Lewis: "There are only
two kinds of people in the end: those who say to God, 'Thy will
be done' and those to whom God says, in the end, 'Thy will be

done.' All that are in hell, choose it. Without that self-choice there could be no hell."[1]

The popular Scottish preacher Alistair Begg seems to say that hell is a choice we make out of sheer stubbornness and an unwillingness to admit when we are wrong: "Would anyone choose Hell over Heaven? YES! Why? Pride. They don't want to go in the only way you can go in, on your knees. They don't want to admit they are a failure, that their life is a mess."[2]

The famous Canadian evangelical theologian J. I. Packer believed something similar: "Scripture sees hell as self-chosen . . . [it] appears as God's gesture of respect for human choice. All receive what they actually chose, either to be with God forever, worshipping him, or without God forever, worshipping themselves."[3]

Wow . . . that's quite a gesture!

What I find interesting about these kinds of statements is that they are working very hard to let God off the hook for hell. It's almost as if they're trying to say, "Don't blame God for hell. God has almost nothing to do with it. It's something that people choose to do to themselves, a natural consequence of rejecting God's love. God just gives us the choice."

It sounds almost as if a hell of eternal torment is not only something that some people *deserve* but that somehow, it's something that people *desire*, that God is simply giving the damned what they *want*. After all, what could be more "just" than giving someone what they're asking for?

I don't know about you, but, for some reason, when I read these kinds of quotes, I can't help but be reminded of the old trope I've seen in countless movies and television shows where an abusive husband has just struck his wife, and then he proceeds to sit down on the bed and blame her for the abuse she suffered at his hands.

"Now look what you made me do," he says.

tainted love

Even coming from an Englishman, a Scotsman, and a Canadian, the argument that the choice between heaven and hell is an expression of human freedom seems tailor-made for an American audience, does it not? After all, America is the land of freedom. America is the place where every cultural issue, every political argument, every social question ultimately boils down to freedom. Here, fiscal conservative politicians don't merely argue against higher taxes or economic regulation; they cry out for "freedom from communism and governmental tyranny." For liberals, it's not enough to say that abortion should be legal. Rather, you have to say that women must have "freedom over their own bodies." Those who oppose abortion do so from a posture of supporting "religious freedom." Even during a global pandemic, statehouses all over the country were flooded with protestors railing against mask mandates and demanding the "freedom to breathe."

Needless to say, if you want to promote an idea in America, it helps if you can argue that it somehow maximizes freedom. If you want to argue for why people should believe in a hell of eternal torment, you have to use the rhetoric of freedom to make it sound like a free choice—like, somehow, those who suffer eternal torment were asking for it all along.

Believe it or not, as a Methodist, this way of looking at heaven and hell makes sense to me, at least on some level. After all, John Wesley, perhaps more than any other theologian, argued that human free will is absolutely essential to Christianity. When he started the Methodist movement, many Protestant Christians believed in the doctrine of predestination, the idea that God chose and predestined everyone who would be saved (and in some iterations, who would be damned) before the beginning of time. At the time, it was thought by many that even if someone seemed to have chosen to become a Christian, it was only because God had

destined them to make that choice in the first place, and if someone was raised in the faith or converted only to later fall away, it
was taken as evidence that perhaps they were never predestined
for salvation to begin with.

Wesley came along and argued that, no, actually God *wants*
everyone to be saved, and that God *draws* all people to salvation,
but that, at the end of the day, God would ultimately respect human free will.[4] God will do everything God can do to attract us,
to beckon us, to *woo* us, but will also let us say "no" to God.

In Methodist theology, this is what makes our love for God
meaningful. After all, if someone is forced to love someone else,
can that even be called "love" at all?

If you had a crush, and instead of asking them out on a date and
doing the hard work of establishing a romantic connection, you
simply slipped some kind of love potion in their drink, wouldn't
you be haunted by the fact that perhaps they never *really* loved you?
Or, consider those who are caught in abusive relationships, who are
made to feel as if they are not free to leave. We would never consider
that to be a *loving* relationship, would we? We would say that it's manipulative and coercive, that there is something inherently wrong
about not respecting someone's choice to *not* be in relationship with
you. It's the choice that makes the love worthwhile. It's the choice
that gives it meaning. It's the choice that makes love, love.

So, as an American and as a Methodist, of course I believe
that the freedom to choose whom to love is important. Without
that choice, love becomes compulsory and abusive, something
that is not love.

But here's the thing: if a relationship is between equals, then
the choice cannot be presented as a threat. If you say someone
has the choice to be in a relationship, yet you threaten to harm
them if they leave, then you haven't given them a choice at all!

That's exactly why I cannot believe that hell is eternal torment or that souls can be somehow "lost" forever and ever. If
God damns us for not believing in God or having a relationship

with God or loving God back, however you want to put it, then that would be the very definition of an abusive relationship. In any other context, that kind of "choice" would be taken as coercive and manipulative, and we would never call it love.

We need a different way to think about our relationship to God. Unlike the relationships we have with friends and romantic partners, our relationship to God is not, after all, one of equals. We give each other the option to opt out of and walk away from relationships because we recognize that our love for one another is fallible and weak, and it always comes laced with heavy doses of insecurity, fear, and ignorance.

Of course, God's love for us is not like that. We believe that we were created to love God. In that sense, then, it seems to me that ultimately God does *force* us into a kind of relationship with God, but God does so without violence or coercion. Rather, unlike the romantic relationships we have with one another, *that* relationship is our natural state, and God simply removes everything that gets in its way.

emancipating beowulf

Consider my dog, Beowulf. In a certain sense, he is my prisoner. Compared to most animals, he has very little actual freedom. He is confined to my house or my office most of the time. Of course, I do let him outside to chase squirrels and bark at leaves, but there's a wooden fence all the way around my backyard to prevent him from escaping. We go for a walk every morning, but I keep him restrained on a leash that's tied to a collar around his neck. If he ever does somehow escape all these measures of control, that same collar has a tag on it with my name and phone number so that if someone finds him, they can turn him in and I can drag him back home, back to where he's safe.

Along with that, I'm not sure that he ever really *chose* to love me. One day my wife and I simply picked him up from a family that couldn't take care of him anymore and we brought him home. He had no say in the matter. He certainly was nervous for the first several days, almost as if he was being kept somewhere against his will, but eventually he warmed up to us and started cuddling with us in bed. I'm sure if he had the power of speech, he would now (hopefully) say that he loved both of us very much, but I suppose his affection could be as much the result of a kind of Stockholm syndrome as anything else.

Tell me, if I opened my front door one day and let him outside to live his life the way he wanted, if I set him loose to go wherever he would like and eat whatever he wanted and chase anything he wanted to chase, would I be making him *more* free?

I would be giving him more *choices*, but, because he lacks the ability to make informed decisions about the consequences of those choices, I would be resigning him to a far worse kind of bondage than he experiences in my home. Instead of the bondage of the leash and the fence, out there, by himself, he would be facing the bondage of hunger, cold, disease, and fear. He would not survive long. Make no mistake, if I simply opened my door and let him wander out wherever he chose, I would be killing him, and that's because I would be offering him a freedom that he was simply never intended to have.

You see, *true* freedom is not simply the dissemination of choice; rather, it is the ability to live and flourish in accordance with one's nature, with who one was created to be.

Beowulf is the result of thousands of years of selective breeding. Down through the centuries, the wolves and dogs that can be counted among his ancestors were chosen to reproduce precisely for their ability to love, work for, and depend upon humans. His reliance on my wife and me is literally written into his DNA. Beowulf, like all of those in his line before him, is designed to have a human master, to live in and through a relationship with a human who cares for him and takes care of his needs. To give him the option to reject that care is not freedom at all. It would be, both legally and morally speaking, criminal neglect.

Oddly, the collar that I keep hooked around Beowulf's neck is a symbol of my love for him. The leash that I use to restrain him is also the leash by which I make him free.

In that way, there's this tiny verse from the Gospel of John that I just can't shake out of my head: "And I, when I am lifted up from the earth, will draw all people to myself" (John 12:32).

To a Methodist, the way this verse has been translated sounds gentle. It makes it seem as if Jesus practices the kind of love we preach about. "He will *draw* us to himself" seems like another way of saying that he will invite us, woo us, do everything he can to charm us with his grace, but at the end of the day, he will still respect our boundaries and autonomy and allow us to walk away if we choose.

That would be great, except, you guessed it, that's a terrible translation. The Greek word here is *helkō*, and it means something much closer to "drag."[5] Elsewhere in the New Testament, we see the word being used to describe the act of hauling heavy nets across the sea floor and up onto a boat and to portray the act of bringing one's legal opponents to court (John 21:6; James 2:6). In the ancient world as in our own, we would never say that we "draw" someone to court. We neither beckon nor invite nor woo them. We compel them to come. We subpoena them. We send police to go and get them. In other words, we *drag* their asses, kicking and screaming if need be.

But if Jesus drags every one of us into heaven, whether we want to go or not, kicking and screaming, as it were, wouldn't he be violating our free will? If everyone must be saved in the end, no matter what, then doesn't that mean that God takes away our freedom?

My answer to that is yes, but only if we define "freedom" in the common American way, as the pure offer of choice, as the opportunity to hurt ourselves infinitely and eternally. But if that is what freedom really is, then why would we want it anyway?

Rather, the fact that God saves everyone eventually is a higher form of freedom, a freedom to be who we were always meant to be and live how we were always meant to live. In the end, we might not have the freedom to walk away from that relationship, but if everything else we say about God is true, then we can be assured that we wouldn't want to.

response-ability

Of course, one could use an argument like this to promote an Orwellian "freedom is slavery" sort of political agenda. The argument that human beings were created to be subservient to special human masters who alone are capable of directing their lives and providing for their needs has been used throughout the centuries to promote all kinds of church inquisitions, absolutist monarchies, dictatorships of the proletariat, and even chattel slavery. But those things are evil for the same reason that turning my dog loose in the modern world would be evil: human beings were not created to be blindingly subservient to one another, and we have an entire history of servitude, colonization, and oppression that speaks to that fact, especially in the church. That kind of life is not in human nature just as much as surviving in a world of busy streets and potentially poisonous garbage is not in Beowulf's.

What we *were* created for, however, is to live under the tender lordship of Christ. That, as much as anything else, is what it means to be made in the "image of God," to be called "children of God." Just as Beowulf was created to spend his days receiving love from Maggie and me, so we are created to receive grace and love from God. That is our natural state, the condition for which we were "bred" by God.

For God to give us the option to live outside of that relationship forever and to experience the painful consequences of that state for all eternity without even the release of death would not be a "gesture" of respect for human choice.[6] It would be an unimaginable cruelty, akin to letting a child play with fire or allowing someone with certain severe developmental disabilities to live outside of a caregiver's watchful gaze. That's because true, actual freedom is dependent not only upon having a choice but also upon having the proper knowledge to make an informed decision and the sanity to recognize the consequences of that decision.[7]

Freedom requires a kind of responsibility—literally, a response-ability, the ability to understand the consequences of one's actions and respond well to them. We don't allow children to play with fire because they do not know that it will invariably harm them and those around them. In the same way, we do not allow people with particularly serious cognitive impairments to live without proper supervision because they may not understand the consequences of their actions. To do so would not be freedom in any sense of the word.

From a certain perspective, we are all spiritually impaired. We have the stain of sin that clouds our judgment. We have emotional and psychological baggage, we have been raised in specific cultures by specific people, and we have brains that are anchored in sensitive biological material and chemicals that can all too easily be thrown out of balance. All these factors have a part to play in all of our decision making, including especially the decisions we make about our faith. This is part of what it means to be finite, to be less than God.

To offer human beings, in all their finitude and psychological vulnerability, the choice to make a decision that could lead to an infinitely bad outcome would not be offering them a kind of responsible freedom. It would be offering them the opportunity to make a mistake the consequences of which they could not possibly be expected to shoulder themselves, at least not in any moral sense. It would be like giving a five-year-old your car keys and, as she tears down the road hitting mailboxes and swerving to avoid pedestrians, yelling after her, "Make good choices!"

Any choice that has infinite consequences cannot be called freedom when it is presented to a finite creature.

bad choices

It becomes clear just how absurd this "freedom of choice" is when it is pulled out of the abstract realm of theology and spirituality and put into the context of the real world. For instance, if I were to offer you a choice between heroin or methamphetamine, I haven't somehow increased your total level of freedom, have I? By giving you that choice at all I've only offered you different kinds of bondage. The mere presence of a choice does not mean that one has offered freedom.

Now, let's say I offer you an even more absurd choice: I can give you a million dollars *or* I can break your arm. It's up to you.

Here we have a choice between something that is, at least on its face, a choice between something good and something bad. But the bad option is so *obviously* bad that it makes one wonder why I've offered it to you in the first place.

I suppose there might be reasons someone would choose to have their arm broken. Perhaps they think I'm joking and want to call my bluff. Perhaps they are rich and would rather not have their taxable income kicked into a higher bracket. Or perhaps they're just a glutton for pain. There are myriad reasons why someone might rather have their arm broken than receive a million dollars, and we can argue about how rational those reasons might be (and whether a person who passes up a million bucks to have their arm broken might actually *deserve* to have their arm broken).

What is inarguable, however, is that it would be wrong of *me* to offer you that choice. It would be wrong of me to create a situation whereby you could choose an outcome that would result in me doing some kind of violence to you. For me to present that choice to you at all would not only be terribly odd but also morally irresponsible.

To believe that God offers us the choice between everlasting bliss and unlimited torture is to say something very dark about the character of God.

Beyond that, broken arms heal. Those who believe in true damnation tell us that it never ends. Who, having been convinced that hell is real and truly knowing, believing, and understanding that it meant everlasting torture, the worst possible fate, would actually choose that path? By that same token, who would not choose God and an eternal life of everlasting bliss? If the options were laid out plainly, if the consequences were made abundantly clear, and if the one doing the choosing had no psychological or cognitive impairments, then a soul would simply be unable to choose anything other than God and heaven. To choose otherwise would be fundamentally irrational and evidence of the fact that the one doing the choosing should have never been offered the choice in the first place.

No amount of pride or stubbornness could ever compel someone to walk into a hell of eternal fire of their own free volition, and it certainly couldn't get them to stay there! Are we to think that those who are in hell continue to reject the mercy of God, or are we to believe that they do repent after they experience the pain of hell and that God, for some reason, no longer accepts their repentance and rejects a relationship with them? Are we to imagine that there are billions of souls crying out for mercy right now, confessing their sin, pleading to have a relationship with God, and God simply ignores them and continues to torture them anyway?

spiritual privilege

By saying that the choice is up to you, preachers and theologians oversimplify the human condition and disregard the very good reasons some people might have to reject the God of Jesus. I know that this may come as a shock to some people, but as a Christian and as a pastor, I recognize that there are good, rational, and totally understandable reasons that people have to reject God. There are those who experience abuse at the hands of clergy, those who have been members of highly controlling religious sects, those who have been victims of religious violence, those who have trauma from religious families, those who have only been exposed to the hateful rhetoric of judgmental Christians, those who have been raised in a different spiritual tradition, or those who have lived their entire lives within and have had their minds shaped by a materialistic culture that simply has no room in its worldview for the existence of a supernatural Trinitarian God . . . just to name a few.

All these examples (and plenty more) might very well present intellectual and psychological challenges to Christian belief that our tender, fleshy, human mind simply cannot overcome in this world. I'm not saying that the church should write them off, stop evangelizing, or stop spreading the message of Jesus's love for the world. I'm simply saying that we must admit to ourselves and to the world that, in this life, there are some who will never come to Christ, and that's all right.

To pretend that religion is a level playing field whereby everyone has the same choice and opportunity to find saving faith in Jesus Christ is about as reasonable as saying that in America, everyone has the same opportunity to find financial success.

In fact, that's probably why "the choice is up to you" plays so well in American evangelical theology. It is the same approach that our culture has toward capitalism and the so-called American meritocracy. They both rely on the same fundamental fallacies: everyone starts from the same place, everyone has the same opportunity, and therefore everyone is equally responsible for the consequences of their choices.

What so many evangelical pastors and theologians fail to recognize, in matters of faith as well as in matters of finance, is that some of us are only where we are because we were born into a kind of privilege. I was born into a family that took its faith seriously; that raised me in the church, gave me money to go to church camp, and supported me when I chose to study theology full time. I have lived my entire life in a culture that (despite what one might hear within Christian nationalist discourse) has been generally approving of the Christian religion. I was fortunate enough to never receive any abuse at the hands of clergy, and even when I did experience unhealthy church leadership, the effects of their disfunction were mitigated by the presence of healthy, loving Christians who kept me in the fold.

When I'm honest with myself and I take those privileges into account, I can't possibly think that I somehow *deserve* my own salvation, even on the basis of faith alone. I certainly have no moral ground to point to those who didn't have those same privileges and say that they somehow deserve an everlasting punishment at the hands of a vengeful God because they *chose* not to believe.

Some will try to refute what I've said so far with Scripture: "for the Lord does not see as mortals see; they look on the outward appearance, but the Lord looks on the heart" (1 Sam. 16:7). But that's exactly my point. If by "heart" we mean the deepest possible place of a person's soul, that God only judges the most fundamental part of who we are, then we can be assured that all will be saved. Why? Because when we drill down that far into who we are, if we inspect the DNA of our souls, even those of the most terrible villains among us, we find that the deepest possible place is not sin. It is not rebellion. It is not stubbornness nor even pride. The deepest part of who we are remains the *imago Dei*, the stained yet never-broken image of God in which we were first created. That is the part of us that makes us worth saving in the first place, and it is the hard, resistant kernel of divinity within each of us that cannot ever be destroyed.

Everything that we call "sin" is merely the hull of human experience. It is the calcified deposition of the sum total of our ignorance, our fear, and the cumulative effect of all our terribly fallen choices within a terribly fallen world that overlays that seed of Godness that was always intended to grow into bloom. It is the slag that covers the golden nugget of who we really are, and no doubt, some of us have much more gunk than others. But it's not who we are, even for the worst among us. It's not the deepest part of our identity. It's dross, and there's no reason to think that God can't burn it all away. When that happens, the part of us that was created in the divine image, the part of us that has been bred to have a relationship with God, will come home, not kicking and screaming but running and panting until we are safe in our Master's house.

eleven

a generous heresy

Thou shalt not be overcome. All shall be well and all
shall be well and all manner of things shall be well.

—The Resurrected Christ,
through St. Julian of Norwich,
Revelations of Divine Love

et's take a moment and ask, So where do we go from here? If
we are convinced that hell is not eternal, that most Christians
for most of time have been wrong about the afterlife, that all are
saved eventually, that the fires of Gehenna are *holy* in that they
are cleansing and purgative, purifying us for an eternity with God,
and that one day even Satan and his demons will be saved by
Christ, what then do we do?

Personally, I think the first thing on our agenda should be to
take a nice, deep breath and *relax.*

To be a Christian universalist is not merely to believe that we
are saved from hell itself—indeed, we all may experience something of the purgative flames of Gehenna—but it is also to believe
that we are saved from the *dread* of hell, the dread we might feel on
our own behalf and, indeed, the dread we might feel for the whole
human race. We know that whatever pain may wait for us on the

other side of death can only be temporary and for the purpose of healing any unresolved spiritual sickness that we would otherwise carry with us into eternity. The first task of the nascent universalist, then, is to take the time to reconcile herself to the idea that, in the most ultimate sense possible, everything will be truly OK. Yet, even this is a more profound experience than it might seem.

Throughout my time in ministry I've had the opportunity to know several women who have been emancipated from abusive husbands, and in nearly all of those cases, they report that there is a moment, when they're in a safe place and they are surrounded by people they love, that something gives way inside of them. After they've packed the car, snuck out in the middle of the night, and found a friend or a sister to stay with—sometime after all that, it dawns on them for the first time that they are free, that they are out of harm's way, and that what they do, how they act, and the way they live need no longer be dictated by the whims of the capricious punisher who had come to dominate their lives. While this awareness of their newfound freedom often comes on slowly, it nevertheless seems to reach a climax where there is a palpable release of fear and anxiety. Tears often flow. A period of deep, heavy sleep ensues. It's almost as if the mind, the body, and the heart are somehow reset, or perhaps reborn.

In the wake of this realization, they might change careers, get new hobbies, start chasing new passions, or begin forming new relationships. Sometimes their life opens up into a limitless horizon of possibility, and it becomes something that they never could have anticipated. Yet before any of that could happen, they first had to mentally recognize, physically accept, and spiritually acknowledge their emancipation. This reconciliation is, necessarily, a profound and holistic experience, and one that ought not be rushed.

Even if we don't think about it consciously, many of us have been carrying around the hell of eternal torment in the back of our minds for our whole lives, wondering about the fate of dead

loved ones, anxious over the destiny of friends who do not yet believe, and even wondering whether we *really* believe, or whether
we believe *enough* to be saved from the worst possible eternity.
For most of us, the immensity of that fear goes unacknowledged
most of the time, living somewhere between our subconscious
and a running list of topics verboten to polite Christian conversation; yet its gravity still pulls on almost every aspect of who we
are: how we live, worship, relate to friends and family, and build
our churches. If the capricious punisher of an abusive Christianity has now fallen, if we and our loved ones are now *truly* safe,
then we must take some time to consider how our lives will be
different—that is, how our lives will be better.

our new freedom

I have always been very religious, even as a child, and I remember
when I was nine and my grandfather was in the hospital slowly
dying of cancer. He was never a religious man in any sense of the
word. I remember being racked by guilt that he may very well
die without saving faith in Jesus Christ. When I look back on
that time in my life, I regret not being able to be truly *present*
with Grandpa in his waning days and weeks, being distracted by
the thought that perhaps I needed to talk to him about Jesus.
When I visited him in the hospital, I didn't have the courage to
do it. The fact that I never had that conversation haunted me for
years afterward. When he finally died, my tears weren't the sub-
lime pain of a young boy facing death for the first time and losing
his grandfather. They were tears of worry that he would now face
eternal torture and tears of shame that I should have done more
to help him.

How messed up is that? What kind of religion puts the weight of
that kind of responsibility on the shoulders of a nine-year-old?

In the years since, as a member of the clergy, I've found myself
at the bedside of many dying people, and I've never once felt the

need to "save" someone, to have that all-important conversation to make sure that they had "invited Jesus into their heart," to make sure their destiny was secure by saying the "sinner's prayer." Instead, I try to do what I wasn't able to do for my grandfather or the rest of my family: I try to be present. I recognize the holiness of the moment. I bear witness to the love and grief of family members. I pray, hold space, and anoint the dying with oil, blessing them for the mysterious journey that they are about to take. And finally, I comfort those gathered there by assuring them that this person will experience the forgiving and saving grace of Christ.

This may sound macabre, but one of my favorite parts of being an ordained pastor is coming to pray over the dying. I've been present at the deaths of many people, some of whom were "saved" and some of whom may not have had an ounce of faith inside of them, and yet I can report that there's almost always grace to be had at the bedside of someone who is passing away, regardless of their faith commitments.

Family gathers. Tears flow. I've seen estranged siblings reconcile over the bed of a dying parent. I've seen long-lost friends show up and express remorse and be forgiven. I've even heard a surprising amount of laughter as loved ones share memories and quibble over stories. After more than ten years in ministry, I'm still continually amazed at how much healing happens at the bedside of the dying.

When you're actually there, in the room where death is happening, the idea of asking someone if they know Jesus or leading them down the "Romans Road" (ya know . . . *just to make sure*) feels trite and offensive, a failure to recognize both the humility and the majesty of what's taking place before you. Imagining that there is something that I can do in the few moments right before someone dies to completely change the trajectory of their eternity is not only terribly vain and arrogant—as if I'm some sort of superhero who is going to save the day at the very last second—

but it's also just plain distracting. Worrying about hell blinds us to the real holiness of death.

By that same token, it can also blind us to the real *tragedy* of death.

A number of years ago, a family friend lost her year-old daughter to a fatal household accident. Walking into the funeral, I had never before felt such a heavy pall of grief over such a large group of people. In that space, before that tiny casket, it was as if we were all united in our acknowledgment that this is one of the worst possible moments any human community could experience: the senseless death of a child.

The Baptist preacher performing the service then got up and told us that although we couldn't understand it, this was all part of God's plan and that we should be *happy* that this child had been chosen to experience the bliss of heaven before having reached something called "the age of accountability," which I took to mean the minimum age required to be subject to the possibility of damnation. He then proceeded to lead us all in the "sinner's prayer" and invited each of us to ask Jesus to come into our heart so that someday we too could bypass the fires of hell and join in heaven the soul of the "little angel" lying before us.

That was the most tone-deaf, insensitive, and just plain irresponsible act of pastoral malpractice I had ever seen. Instead of acknowledging the tragedy, leading us to work through our grief, and helping us draw closer to God in the midst of an unimaginable darkness, all he could do was slap a "SALVATION" sticker over the whole thing and tell us to be *thankful* that this child narrowly avoided the precarious position of being subject to an eternal hell. He, like so many other pastors, was so obsessed with the dichotomy of heaven and hell that he became blind to everything that happens in between.

Sermons like that are the exact reason that, these days, some decent people can no longer stomach the idea of Christianity.

The problem, of course, is that a hell of eternal torment is obsessive by its very nature. After all, if it's true, and some of us may be headed for an eternity of torment, everything that pastor said that day was not only perfectly appropriate but absolutely necessary. That's how hell threatens to turn us all into narrow-minded, insensitive, and anxious evangelists of a dark gospel that doesn't care for the grace or tragedy of actual human life but instead is preoccupied with avoiding everlasting torture.

When we jettison the idea of hell as it has been handed down to us, we free ourselves to find God in the here and the now, in all the holiness and hardship of human life. Rather than offering anxiety-laden pleas for salvation, we can embrace others in real ministry. When we are able to look at our friends and neighbors— not as souls dangling over Jonathan Edwards's abyss but as God's children navigating a world of pain and grace—then we can be truly present to offer companionship, community, and love.

In that way, consider what our churches might look like if we could get past the overarching task of "saving souls." In the United Methodist Church, we don't often talk explicitly about saving souls from the fires of hell, but it's an implicit goal that affects everything we do. For instance, we can't help but judge the success of our churches based on their size. We mourn when we notice our congregations shrinking and rejoice when they grow. At the end of every year, my conference requires detailed reports, including numbers of those who have been baptized, those who have been confirmed, and those who "profess" saving faith for the very first time. Certainly, any institution will want to take stock of who is involved and how we are touching lives in our community, but all of these metrics hint, even in the most subtle ways, to a tally of saved souls that we imagine exists somewhere in heaven.

Serving the United Methodist Church, a denomination in decline (at least by the metric of our membership and attendance numbers), I've come across so many people who are guilt-ridden because their local church is dying. They feel as if they are failing, as if they are letting down all those neighbors in their community who might go to hell forever just because their church won't be there to save them. In reality, demographics shift. Secularism is rising on a cultural scale. In most cases, the decline of a church has almost nothing to do with the faith or faithlessness of its individual members, but nevertheless, in a world where church effectiveness is measured by the number of souls saved, Christians who have led lives of grace and mercy are made to feel as if they've let down both their God and their neighbor.

That is a burden that is too great for either churches or individuals to bear, and I don't think Jesus ever intended them to.

Now, imagine a church that openly proclaims the ultimate salvation of all people. Imagine a church that is free to serve people where they are, proclaiming the gospel without the constant pressure of proselytization, as if everything relies on the conversion of individuals. Imagine a church that can respond to all the needs of its community without feeling guilty that its numbers have decreased and it hasn't yet saved enough souls. Church consultants often ask leaders to imagine what they could do if money were no object: how they would follow their passions, serve their community, and make the world a better place. Now ask yourself what *your* church could do if hell were no object.

what's the rush?

That being said, I don't have any illusions that someday Christian universalism will be widely accepted as doctrine in my denomination or any other. There are families, churches, entire denominations, and even cultures (perhaps your own) whose very foundations are built on the ideology of an eternal hell. In America, for instance, evangelical Christianity isn't just a religious tradition. It's an industry with profit-motivated interests in publishing, music, and entertainment. Today, megachurches grow not just as spiritual communities but as lifestyle brands with influencers who shape taste and opinion on social media, driving demand for various products and services. And of course, in the last few years, we've all become increasingly aware of the political expression of Christianity, where—just as in Dante's time—politicians use their faith (including the fear of damnation) to posture themselves, gain power from the masses, and exert control over society. The tradition of hell is too long, its psychological power too potent, and its stakeholders too numerous for it to be simply "canceled" or otherwise defeated quickly.

Besides that, we need to realize that we live in a time when, for whatever reason, people seem to like drawing lines in the sand. This is an age of a million revolutions, when people imagine themselves to be putting their foot down, striking their staff to the bridge, and bellowing, "YOU SHALL NOT PASS!"[1] More than ever in my lifetime, people see themselves as being part of movements and rebellions, toppling power structures, deconstructing institutions, all so that something new and better can be raised up in their place.

I personally think that many of these movements are God-breathed and more than overdue, like Black Lives Matter, MeToo, and many others. But I'm not at all convinced that such revolutionary fervor is the answer to every problem. Sometimes the answer to a bad ideology is not simply to replace it with another ideology. Sometimes the answer to a bad ideology is simply the presence of more humility.

That's what all this is about, isn't it?

Christians these days are always talking about things like revivals, revolutions, and reformations; always convincing themselves that they are on the precipice of some wonderfully dramatic pseudo-messianic event that's about to rush into the world; that a massive dam is always just about to break, and a wave of change, growth, and spiritual revitalization will be unleashed upon the world.

It's exciting to think that way. The unfortunate thing, however, is thinking like that can make one short-sighted—and far too certain.

Remember the apostles who, when confronting the controversy of circumcision in the early church, came out and said, "It *seems* to us and to the Holy Spirit . . ." That's the energy of Christian universalism. It's an attitude that can afford *not* to be desperate, a posture of confidence that allows us to calmly consider, discern, and communicate what we *think* the Spirit is saying to the churches, without the ticking clock of eternal damnation making us scurry about like rats trying to find our way from a sinking ship.

If universalists suddenly come out with our ideological guns blazing, canceling those who think differently, shouting down the opposition, and working to enforce our beliefs on our churches and denominations, we would run the risk of falling into that same dualistic- or binary-thinking trap that got us hell in the first place. By splitting the Christian world into two oppositional camps—say, universalist and infernalist—we would end up creating sheep and goats of our own. We would further rupture the body of Christ and actually work against the goals of recognizing just how compassionate and patient God really is and conforming our church communities into that divine image.

To insist that our belief in purgatorial universalism become the dominant and dogmatic view of Christianity would be to work in the spirit and power of an infernalist hell.

practicalities

So, if we aren't necessarily seeking revival, revolution, or reformation on a grand scale (though certainly we wouldn't want to do anything that might oppose such reform), what *can* we do to create meaningful change where we are?

Church leaders will have their work cut out for them, as we, the clerical class, have historically been the worst offenders when it comes to using the fear of an eternal hell to gain influence and wield power.

The first thing that clergy and other leaders can do immediately is to stop using *hell* as the default translation for words like *Gehenna*, *Sheol*, and *Hades*. By swapping in the original Greek or Hebrew word, we can introduce nuance to our sermons and Bible studies and elicit questions for further discussion. This may require some experience with biblical languages, but if all else fails, one can rely on David Bentley Hart's translation of the New Testament, which was written with an eye toward universalism.[2]

However, I don't want to assume that we should banish the word *hell* from our worship vocabulary altogether. For those of us who find ourselves in higher liturgical denominations, we may come across prayers, litanies, and blessings where *hell* might be used. When that happens, there simply is no referent word in Greek or Hebrew. In those cases, I think it's perfectly fine to use *hell*, especially when it's there for dramatic purposes. The truth is that there is something painful on the other side of this life, something to be avoided or at least mitigated by our faithfulness on this side of the grave, and calling that thing *hell* isn't necessarily wrong, as long as we make sure that those under our care know that it's for our own good and that it isn't eternal.

Homiletically, we can preach sermons that carefully deconstruct the eternal hell that has become a default Christian belief. Sermons about the restitution of all things in the *apokatastasis*, the parable of the sheep and the goats, the true meaning of "weeping and gnashing of teeth," and the "pool of fire" from the book of Revelation all provide ample opportunities to explain the universal hope of the gospel and the purgatorial cleansing that takes place for some of us on the other side of death. I've included a sample sermon I've preached to my own congregation in order to demonstrate what a universalist sermon might look like (see the appendix).

What I do *not* recommend, however, is trying to preach one single sermon that will convert the whole of one's congregation to universalism. We are dealing with two thousand years of doctrine and all the cultural assumptions about hell that a majority of the people in church pews take for granted. Trying to account for all the passages of Scripture that are used to promote the idea of an eternal hell, explaining how original languages have been mistranslated, deconstructing the theological infrastructure of the afterlife, and replacing all of it with the hope of the redemption of all things (*apokatastasis*) in one fell swoop, in twenty minutes on a single Sunday morning (or forty-five, if you're an evangelical), is a fool's errand. While you may win the approval of a few compassionate souls who were halfway there already, it's more likely that you will leave a significant portion of your congregation going home confused and defensive. It's simply unfair to ask people to change such an important part of their theological worldview so quickly.

What's better is to introduce the topic slowly and responsibly, using sermons and Bible studies to ask questions, cast doubt on the idea of endless torment, and promote the extravagant compassion of Christ.

After a while, someone may ask you outright for your opinion, and in these situations it's best to be totally honest. If you believe it, then proudly own the title of universalist. Talk slowly, keeping in mind that what you are saying may be totally new to some people. Be confident as you give an account for what you believe and why, but never condemn or dismiss those who think differently. Remember that we are all on a journey and that the great thing about the universal love of Christ is that one doesn't have to believe in it to experience it.

The one place where I think that universalist clergy should be unapologetically blunt and straightforward, however, is during end-of-life care. Those who are facing the loss of a loved one who they fear will face eternal damnation or those who are grieving someone whom they believe to be experiencing torment ought to be comforted with the assurance of universal salvation in the most candid terms possible. Likewise, when asked to perform the funeral rites of someone outside the Christian faith, the forgiveness of sins should be proclaimed frankly and Christ's promise of eternal life should be declared with full-throated confidence.

The moment when we are directly confronted with the reality of death is no time to mince words or tiptoe around theological debates. The stakes are simply too high. The trauma that people can experience while believing that their loved one is facing damnation is so destructive that they should be afforded every hope, promise, and assurance that we clergy can muster to comfort them and assuage their fears.

But clergy aren't the only ones who are responsible for spreading the gospel of Christian universalism.

In many ways, laypeople have a much more difficult task ahead of them. Because it is a minority viewpoint, most of what's been written about Christian universalism is only to be found among the works of academic theologians and philosophers that those without a theological education might find inaccessible. That's part of the reason why I wrote this book—so that laypeople without an academic background would have a resource to start them on their journey toward a universalist faith. But there are several good resources that are both helpful and accessible.

Some might be surprised to learn that there has always been a tradition of Christian universalism, even from the ancient days of the church. The foundations of this view come from Origen of Alexandria's *On the First Principles* and Gregory of Nyssa's *On the Soul and the Resurrection*, though they can be a real slog for those who are unfamiliar with ancient writing styles.

Some folks might not be ready to tackle David Bentley Hart's *That All Shall Be Saved*, which is thought by many to be the definitive modern account of Christian universalism in the English language.[3] The two-volume set *A Larger Hope?* by Ilaria L. E.

Ramelli and Robin A. Parry might present a more manageable challenge to those who are looking to study the long history of universalism within Christianity.[4]

Inventing Hell by Jon M. Sweeney is a great and accessible resource for those who are looking to understand the way hell has been used as a tool of political power throughout history.[5]

Finally, *Dante's Road* by Marc Thomas Shaw is a spiritual masterwork that salvages Dante's framework of heaven, hell, and purgatory by turning it into a spiritual exercise. This book changed my life.[6]

The point is that if you are a Christian universalist, you must "always be ready to make your defense to anyone who demands from you an accounting for the hope that is in you" (1 Pet. 3:15). The bigger the hope, then the more clear that account needs to be because some folks will fight like hell (forgive the pun) to defend damnation. The Christian universalist will be expected to articulate her beliefs again and again, so she would do well to study so that she can confirm with her mind and her words what she already knows in her heart. I truly believe that there is something inside all of us that resonates with universalism, if for no other reason than that we love Christ and know just how loving and compassionate he is. The hard part is putting that feeling into words, discovering its logical framework, and finding it in Scripture.

As I've tried to demonstrate, universalism *is already* in Scripture. The problem is that it's covered over by millennia of poor translations and misguided theology. I hope this book has shown you that all it takes is some work and a little perseverance to dust it off.

For the laypeople who are reading this, allow me to let you in on a little secret: some of us clergy love to be challenged. Those of us who are immature and insecure might bristle or even condemn those who confront us with alternatives to the theological status quo, but those are the clergy who probably aren't worth following in the first place. Most of us love it when one of our parishioners brings up a contrary point in Bible study or after the service, especially if they can back up their point with sound reasoning.

If you want to shock your priest or minister, impress her with your knowledge of Greek and Hebrew. From my perspective as a pastor, presenting me with a respectful argument to something I say or preach is a great way of letting me know that you are engaging my words, that you are taking your faith seriously, and that you care about your own spirituality. On a few occasions, I've even had parishioners offer to take me out to coffee to discuss some theological topic or question they have. That's the kind of church work I *always* have time for.

The main thing that all of us need to remember is that universalists are the ones who are supposed to have more hope than anyone. When you're trying to build hope, rarely do arrogance, condemnation, or competitiveness make for effective tools.

I've been arguing (sometimes respectfully, sometimes not) over theology for decades now, and I've never once had more hope because someone told me I was wrong. However, I can remember many times that my hope increased and I was encouraged to keep seeking and talking and asking questions, all because someone told me I wasn't yet right *enough*. The Christians in our pews and pulpits are absolutely right when they talk about how great Jesus is. It's just that when they also talk about a hell of eternal torment, they aren't yet right enough.

the generous heretic

The final question we must ask is the one where, unfortunately, most people begin: Is Christian purgatorial universalism a heresy?

It's sad to me that this question is the starting point for many who simply presuppose that universalism must be heresy and then tie themselves in theological knots defending the idea that certainly God must either torment souls for all eternity or, if they want to take the "free-will" defense, argue that God doesn't do absolutely everything God can do to prevent our ignorant souls from making the worst possible mistake. We wonder why the reputation of our religion is so bad while we bend ourselves over backward trying to find ways to make the case that either (a) God hates some people so much that God tortures them forever and ever or (b) God is somehow so *disinterested* in humanity that God would allow us to stumble into hell the same way a child might stumble into traffic.

There's a popular meme that constantly makes the rounds in universalist spaces online, with a famous picture of Jesus knocking on a door, and he says, "Let me in so I can save you." A voice from inside asks, "Save me from what?" Jesus replies, "From what I'm going to do to you if you don't let me in."

It's this exact kind of spiritual blackmail that thoughtful people no longer have time for, and instead of interrogating the doctrine that produces it, theologians, pastors, and Christian influencers often do everything they can to defend it and call those who deny an eternal hell—you guessed it—heretics.

So, it's at least worth asking, Are we heretics?

Let me first say that most of us are not so arrogant as to count ourselves or our belief among the world-shaking doctrines known as the "Great Heresies" or among those hugely influential teachers and villains of history known as the "Arch-Heretics."

When you study the history of Christian thought, it becomes apparent that in the early centuries of Christian doctrine, the term *heresy* wasn't applied to just any old bad teaching. Heresy isn't merely wrong. For instance, someone could claim that Jesus was actually a group of penguins stacked on top of one another inside of a trench coat. No one would take the time to call that a heresy. There would be no council called to discuss it, no bishop would bother excluding such a person from communion, and no anathema would be pronounced. It would be written off as silly and ignored.

Likewise, in the mainline Protestant world, we have all kinds of quibbles over doctrines and practices (Calvinism vs. Arminianism, the sprinkle vs. the dunk, etc.), and some of these are enough to split us off from one another, but rarely would you find Protestants who are willing to question whether differences in those finer points of faith might constitute actual, damnable heresy. In fact, within the decline of our current religious climate, you would be hard-pressed to find pastors who would actually push a living, breathing person out of the pew because they didn't perfectly align with their church's doctrine.

No, true heresy is something different. While there's no universal definition of Christian heresy, when one looks over the history of the doctrine of the church, a few identifying marks begin to emerge.

For one, heresies not only challenge important doctrine (what Catholics and the Orthodox might call *dogma*) but they do so in a way that is *compelling* and that gathers a large following. True heresies aren't just weird ideas that float around the Christian landscape and get passed around at coffee hour after service. True heresies shake the Christian world. The destructive thing about them is that they are accessible enough to make sense to people. They are plausible enough to ring true and attractive enough to be popular. Heresy doesn't spark and fizzle. Heresy burns. It catches like wildfire, so much so that it usually takes some sort of official administrative act of condemnation to put it out.

Likewise, heresy isn't confined to a mere point of detail, even though it may start there; it portends a greater, more holistic threat. Heresy is seen as dangerous because if widely accepted, it would result in *sea change* in the nature of what it is to be called *Christian*. It would affect not only theology but also spirituality, worship, and ethics. Heresies are potential *paradigm shifts* in the way Christianity is understood, not granular points of disagreement.

Finally, heresy often has a *political* component, one that challenges the practical direction of the church or threatens to create a change that is intolerable to the status quo. The ancient heresy of Arianism, for instance, endangered the unity of the church within the Roman Empire that was so important to Saint Athanasius and Emperor Constantine that a council had to be called and it had to be publicly condemned for the good of the church and for the good of the empire. In the same way, the desire to include queer people in the full life of the church is often treated like a modern-day heresy (even though the debate mostly hangs on how a mere handful of Bible verses are interpreted) because it calls into question the social and cultural positions that many conservative denominations have staked out in the current political landscape. The potentially damaging effects of heresy aren't limited to the church itself but often escape out into the realities of the wider world.

So how does Christian purgatorial universalism stack up?

I'm afraid that it is not now nor has it ever seemed to have a large enough following to earn a spot among the great heresies. Universalism has always been an undercurrent within Christianity, and it has often been suppressed, but to my knowledge it has never reached such a critical mass of popularity that it needed to be addressed administratively by the church as a whole.[7]

As to the second point, I think it's obvious that universalism does cause such a reevaluation of who God is, who Christians are called to be, and the very nature of existence itself such that, if it were to catch fire in a meaningful way, it would present challenges to our status quo that many church leaders would find intolerable.

The universalist will always believe that the character of God is *necessarily* more compassionate, more patient, and more concerned with the ultimate destiny of individuals than other Christians will admit. Universalists will always give more attention to the idea that "God is love" than those who will continue to insist that God either damns or allows people to be damned. In studying theology, I've often been told that we must "balance

God's compassion with God's justice" or "weigh God's love for humankind with God's hatred for sin." Universalists will always reject that kind of equilibrium, and that will change not only our theology but also our identity. If we imagine ourselves to be made in the image of a universalistic God, we will become universalistic people, and that will change how we live our lives in definite and political ways, opening us up to the ire of those in power.

One of the most popular critiques of universalism is that it would destroy the practice of evangelism. After all, why would we work hard to save the lost if no one is truly lost in the first place?

Well, yeah. That's exactly right. For centuries, Christians have been working very hard indeed—working hard at threatening, shaming, and even colonizing people, all in the name of "saving" them. Converting the masses has always been treated as this ultimate act of love, one that excuses whatever other harms and indignities we might visit upon them along the way. In this way, evangelism has always been a suitable mask for darker imperial, capitalist, and racist impulses. Universalists will reject that kind of evangelism every time. To us, evangelism will have lower stakes. It will always occupy a lower rung on our ladder of priorities, and we will never be convinced that we should sacrifice loving our neighbor in the name of "saving" them.

In that way, universalism may not *destroy* evangelism, but it would *reshape* it beyond all recognition. Instead of doing everything possible to move souls from one category to another, we can acknowledge that when it comes to standing before God, we all exist on a spectrum. Under that framework, evangelism means doing what you can to help people move closer to God in the here and now, while having the quiet confidence to acknowledge that ultimately God will close the gap for everyone. The evangelists of a universalistic Christianity will practice their craft with all the love they can muster but leave behind the anxiety-inducing manipulation of the ticking clock. For us, the salvation of an individual soul will never be an emergency. That means we will never be tempted to compromise the ethics of Christ for the goal of creating more Christ followers. It means that we would rather allow someone to pass through this life rejecting Jesus than become the reason that they reject him.

Finally, as to the third point, universalism also completely changes the way a Christian thinks about politics. We are going to want to see people treated with the same kind of long-suffering compassion with which God treats us. We are going to draw fewer lines in the sand. We are going to reject labels and boundaries. We will refuse to demonize our political and cultural opponents, and we will choose paths that favor peace, compassion, and understanding far more often than what the current status quo will be able to tolerate.

If God refuses to condemn, so will we. If God makes room for everyone, so will we. If God gives all the riches of the kingdom to those who do not deserve it, so will we.

When we search for truth in the Methodist tradition, we like to follow something we call the Wesleyan Quadrilateral. We articulate this with four words: Scripture, tradition, experience, and reason. If something is true in a theological sense, then we believe it must (1) be found in Holy Scripture, (2) be represented in Christian tradition, (3) comport with our experience of lived faith, and (4) be found to be rationally defensible. This is the way that we Methodists determine whether a theological claim is truly orthodox, and in this book, my aim has been to show that what I call purgatorial universalism checks all four boxes.

Yet most of my brothers, sisters, and siblings have not even heard of such an idea, and many of them, I suspect, might reject it on face value.

But at the same time, I have to admit that universalism is nowhere near popular or influential enough to be an "according-to-Hoyle" heresy. It is not yet perceived to be an earth-shattering threat to the status quo of institutional Christianity. As of now, universalism does not yet haunt the nightmares of the powers and principalities of our political elite . . .

But it's always good to have something to shoot for.

If the day ever comes that universalism does become a troublesome groundswell within Christianity, if it ever does start to change the church and her practices from the bottom up, and if it ever begins to shake the corridors of political power, then maybe that title will come. If that does happen, then I hope we will wear the moniker with pride. It seems to me that I'd rather be known as a heretic who believes in an overly generous God than as a fully orthodox disciple of damnation.

For now, perhaps it's enough to say that "it *seems* good, to us and to the Holy Spirit," to declare the salvation of all.

heaven buddies

a sample christian universalist sermon

Here is a sermon (with a few edits for the sake of publication) that I delivered on March 27, 2022, to Uniontown United Methodist Church in northeast Ohio, the congregation I was serving at the time. I offer it to you here as a sample of what a Christian universalist sermon can look like in a mainline Protestant context. The congregation to which it was delivered was in no way radical or even all that progressive. It was a politically and theologically "purple" congregation in a relatively blue-collar Rust Belt town. Yet the sermon struck a chord. From the remarks I received on it afterward, the kind of assurance I was trying to offer the congregation that day was warmly received with gratitude and relief. To me, this sermon represents the deep hunger that Christians feel to be told that in the end, everything will be OK. Themes from this sermon also appear in chapter 6, especially under "Heaven Buddies." In quotations of Scripture, emphasis is my own.

SCRIPTURE LESSONS:
  2 Corinthians 5:16–21
  Luke 15:11–31, "The Prodigal Son"

Sometimes things just aren't the same without that one special person.

In my first year of seminary down in North Carolina, my friend Scott asked me if I wanted to play golf with him and his friends. They had a free guest pass to a local country club. Since I had never played on a private course before, I jumped at the chance. I remember heading out on that first tee, with my clubs and my shoes, getting to ready to have some fun, but the whole enterprise just felt somehow off, like something wasn't quite right. By the time we got some drinks between the ninth and the tenth holes, I had figured it out. In all my years of playing golf, since I was eleven years old, this was the first time I had ever played a round without either my father or my big brother being with me.

I still remember how they taught me the game: my father showing me how to swing in the backyard, my brother instructing me in the finer points of course etiquette. We would go to the driving range on Saturday mornings. We played in a league on Thursday nights. Sometimes I would play with my dad, and sometimes I would play with my brother, or sometimes we would all play together, but there was *never* a time that I went golfing without one of them being there.

And let me tell you, playing with those other guys in North Carolina, I was just awful. I couldn't hit a drive or sink a putt to save my life, and when, on the eighteenth green, I had finally put a decent hole together and scored a birdie, I couldn't really even enjoy it. Even as the other guys gave me high fives and pats on the back, it felt somehow empty or meaningless—all because neither my dad nor my brother was around to see it. They were my golf buddies. I guess sometimes things just aren't the same without that special person.

I think that's what happens when you really love somebody, when you know you've made that connection. Their absence just sort of blocks your experience of something you should like. Even when you know something should be good, it just isn't good if they aren't there to share it with you. At the end of the day, it just doesn't feel right.

* * *

I think that kind of absence is what makes it really hard when people just up and leave a church, isn't it? Sometimes there are folks who are part of a church family, who engrain themselves in the life of the church, and then one day, they just sort of stop showing up without telling anyone or saying goodbye. I know that they think they have their reasons and that they think that it's their business and their business alone, but what they don't realize is that after we've grown so close to them, their absence hurts and things just aren't the same without them.

If you've ever lost a parent or a spouse or, God forbid, a child, you know exactly what I'm talking about, right? There are certain places, events, holidays, whatever that just lose something because that loved one isn't there to enjoy them with you. Have you had an experience like that? Sure, you can move on with your life and the grief becomes more manageable, but at the end of the day there are certain things that just feel, well, *wrong* without that one special person by your side.

So then, what about heaven?

* * *

You may find this hard to believe, but in my job as a preacher, I don't really talk about heaven and hell that much. And I know that's strange, that there are some preachers who *only* talk about heaven and hell, but for the life of me, I can't remember the last time I gave a sermon where I pontificated about the golden streets of Kingdom Come or the sulfurous fires of damnation itself. But I know that in everyone's mind, it's there, somewhere, just offstage, just behind the scenes, and every once in a while, it comes to the fore.

Years ago, I was talking to a parishioner from a different church, just shooting the breeze, and then out of nowhere she told me that she was scared to death that her departed father was burning in hell. I said, "Why would you ever think that?" And she said that her dad wasn't particularly bad or anything. In fact, she loved him very much, but he just wasn't very religious. He didn't really talk about Jesus or anything like that. He didn't go to church. And after he died, one day a member of her own family told her that he was probably in hell. And this woman was crying right in front of me and I didn't know what to say. I mean, what do you say to someone who has not only lost a parent on earth but who thinks that their parent is somehow going to be tortured forever and ever? What do you say to someone who is actually afraid to go to heaven because they don't want to get there only to find out that their loved one isn't anywhere to be found?

I don't think I said anything at all helpful to that woman that day, but if I had it all to do over again, I would have asked her whether she was planning on going to heaven. And if she said yes, then I would have told her about playing golf without my dad and my brother, and I would have told her that if it's true that some things just aren't the same without that one special person, then it must be true in heaven too. If heaven is pure joy, if heaven is the bliss of God in all his glory, then it must necessarily include those people without whom heaven just wouldn't be heaven for you. Now that was a clunky sentence, so let me put it plain: If you are going to spend eternity with God in heaven, and heaven just can't be heaven without that one special person—a spouse, a friend, a sibling, a child, whoever—then that means they must be there too.

* * *

Think about it like this: let's say I won a trip to Disney World, but my wife came down with something painful—I don't know, shingles or hemorrhoids or something like that—and she had to stay home. Could I even enjoy Disney World without her? I mean, what kind of person would I be, having a great time, riding Space Mountain, It's a Small World, Thunder Canyon, eating funnel cakes, all of it, knowing that she was back at home, walking funny, sitting gingerly on one of those weird pillows, can't get comfortable . . .

That would be awful, right? I would be a jerk of a husband if I did that. OK, maybe I would be *more* of a jerk of a husband if I did that. So then how could any one of us possibly enjoy eternity knowing that any of our most precious loved ones were burning forever and ever?

A lot of theologians have tried to answer that question over the years, and some have said, "Well, maybe when you're in heaven, your mind will be so overwhelmed with grace and beauty and happiness that you won't even *think* about where your loved ones are. It won't even occur to you to worry about them."

Wait, so you're telling me that I'll be so *self-absorbed* in the fun I'm having in heaven, I'll be so high, essentially, that I'll forget all about everyone who meant anything to me in life? Wouldn't that mean that I was being somehow *less* compassionate than I am now? Wouldn't that mean that I have more love in my heart *now*, on this side of the grave, than I will when I'm in heaven? That's not what I signed up for. That's not how this is supposed to work.

Likewise, I found another theologian who said, "Well, maybe God 'touches the mind' of the glorified soul, so they can't even remember those who are burning in hell."

Oh, so now you're telling me that I have to be *lobotomized* before I go to heaven, that I have to have my memories and my care and my desire for my loved ones cut out of my mind?

No! That's not what I want! I want all my memories, I want all my love, I want all my friends and loved ones with me, right by my side. *I want them!* The same way that a game of golf just isn't a game of golf without my dad and my brother, so heaven just wouldn't be heaven without certain people. My dad and my brother are my golf buddies, but they are also my *heaven* buddies, you know? Along with my wife and my mom and my sister and my dogs, right? I don't care how much they go to church. I don't care what religion they are. I think my dog Beowulf might be a Zoroastrian or something, but I don't care about that. I can't be blissful knowing that they are in pain. If any one of them is damned, I will be damned too. And I know they feel the same way about me. That means that if any one of us is to be saved, we must all be saved.

* * *

I know each of you has someone to whom you are connected like this, a heaven buddy, so to speak. You have a heaven buddy, don't you? Can you picture that person in your mind right now? Someone without whom you could never find eternal rest because you cannot rest knowing that they are in trouble? In fact, I'm guessing that you probably have more than one, and I bet all of them have their own heaven buddies, and so on and so forth, spreading out in every possible direction—ties of love, like mountain climbers, connected waist to waist, heart to heart, towing one another up the same towering peak, toward the same God, seeking out the same heavenly summit. Sure, some may stumble from time to time, some may even tumble down the face of the rock and hurt themselves and bring a few with them, but ultimately *no one* can fall all the way down because we are all connected. Might I propose that it may even be the case that the whole world is caught up in this web of love and mutuality and collective destiny.

You heard it from Paul in 2 Corinthians: "In Christ, God was reconciling the *world* to himself." It wasn't, "In Christ, God was reconciling, um, let's see, the Methodists, and the Catholics (the good ones anyway), and, uh, maybe the Lutherans to himself, and . . . that's about it. That's the end of the line. Cut it there." No, that's ridiculous. Is it really so crazy to think that when Paul says that God has reconciled the world, maybe, just maybe he means the *whole* world?

This kind of reminds me of Romans 5:18, where Paul says, "Just as one man's trespass led to condemnation for all, so one man's act of righteousness leads to justification and life *for all*."

You'll have to forgive me. I'm not very good with words. Does *all* mean *all*, or does *all* mean *some*?

Or consider Romans 11:32: "for God has imprisoned *all* in disobedience so that he may be merciful to *all*." There's that word again. All. All. All. Can *all* really mean *all* if it's found in the Bible? Does the Bible have some sort of different definition of that word than the rest of us? I don't know about you, but it seems to me that when a lot of Christians say *all*, what they really mean is *some*, or *a few*, or more specifically, *the few who look, think, act, and talk as I do*. Now I know that you're not supposed to prooftext. You're not supposed to just lift just one little verse out of the Bible and use it to prove your point. That's wrong. That's irresponsible. I'm sorry.

But for what it's worth, 1 Corinthians 15:22 says, "for as *all* die in Adam, so *all* will be made alive in Christ"; and let us not forget Titus 2:11: "For the grace of God has appeared, bringing salvation to *all*."

Vicar Derek! Stop it this instant! What are you saying here? That everyone goes to heaven eventually? That . . . that's heresy! To say that at the end of the day all of humanity, from across all of space and time, will one day bow down before God in submission and grace, that at the name of Jesus every knee will bend, in heaven and on earth and under the earth, and that every tongue shall confess that Jesus Christ is Lord to the glory of God the Father?! Is that what you're saying?!

Well, yeah, but that's not heresy; it's just Philippians 2:10–11.

Folks, I'm not telling you that you can't believe in hell. You can believe in hell all you want. The only thing I'm telling you is that you can't believe in a stingy God. I'm just telling you that you can't be the older brother who burns with resentment that the younger brothers who spend their lives in futility and wastefulness are still loved by their Father. You can't believe that God would so easily spend eternity without his children, and you can't believe that God might be so powerless that God can't save anyone God wants to save.

* * *

Years ago I was talking to my dad about heaven, and he said, "Well, I sure do hope there's golf up there."

I said, "Oh, why is that?"

I thought he was joking, but he was as serious as a heart attack. He said, "Because I can't imagine that it would be heaven without golf." Golf was so fun and meaningful to him. It was the way he connected with his boys and his friends and even his own father back in the day. Heaven just wouldn't be heaven without it.

Now I don't know whether there will be golf in heaven, but what I do know is that whatever heaven is, you'll be there, and my dad and my brother will be there, and I will too, eventually, because I don't think God can imagine a heaven without you, or them, or me, or even the worst person any of us can think of. You have your heaven buddies, and I have mine, but if you ask me, I think deep down, one day, one way or another, we'll all be hittin' the links with Jesus, because to him, we are all that one special person.

notes

chapter two

1. "Belief in Hell," Pew Research Center, accessed April 12, 2023, https://www.pewresearch.org/religion/religious-land scape-study/belief-in-hell/.

2. Dante Alighieri, *The Inferno*, trans. Henry Francis Cary (Chicago: Charles C. Thompson, [1866]), 30.

3. Dante, *Inferno*, 87.

chapter three

1. I say "he" because fire-and-brimstone preachers tend to come from churches and traditions that do not recognize the ordination of women.

2. Or as it is sometimes rendered, Niflheim.

3. Actually, there was a fiery opposite to Niflhel in Norse cosmology. It was called Muspelheim, but it had nothing to do with either the souls of the dead nor their torture. Where the cold from Niflhel meets the hot lava of Muspelheim is where the sparks that created the sun and stars were born.

chapter four

1. Ilaria L. E. Ramelli, *A Larger Hope?*, vol. 1, *Universal Salvation from Christian Beginnings to Julian of Norwich* (Eugene, OR: Cascade, 2019), 197.

2. Jonathan Edwards, "Sinners in the Hands of an Angry God," sermon, July 8, 1741, *Blue Letter Bible*, https://www.blueletterbible .org/Comm/edwards_jonathan/Sermons/Sinners.cfm.

3. Mark Driscoll, "Jesus Sweats Blood," sermon, October 9, 2011, *Real Faith*, https://realfaith.com/sermons/jesus-sweats-blood/.

4. "Limp-wristed" is one of Mark Driscoll's favorite homophobic terms to refer to those whose doctrine of hell is not robust enough to satisfy his instinct for violence.

5. Phyllis Tickle, *The Great Emergence: How Christianity Is Changing and Why* (Grand Rapids: Baker, 2012), 13–31.

chapter five

1. Ilaria L. E. Ramelli, *A Larger Hope?*, vol. 1, *Universal Salvation from Christian Beginnings to Julian of Norwich* (Eugene, OR: Cascade, 2019), 16.

2. Samuel Wells, "Refiner's Fire," sermon, December 10, 2006.

3. Hilarion Alfeyev, *Christ the Conqueror of Hell* (Crestwood, NY: St. Vladimir's, 2009), 204.

4. Alfeyev, *Christ the Conqueror of Hell*, 204.

5. Alfeyev, *Christ the Conqueror of Hell*, 78, 163–64. This includes the Eastern theologians particularly of the Alexandrian tradition, particularly Cyril, Clement, Origen, and Athanasius the Great.

6. As quoted from the octoechos, liturgical hymns from Eastern Orthodoxy in Hilarion Alfeyev, *Christ the Conqueror of Hell*, 168–71, emphasis mine.

7. William Williams, translated from the Welsh by Peter Williams and the author, "Guide Me, O Thou Great Jehovah," in *The United Methodist Hymnal* #127. Emphasis mine.

8. Martin Luther, translated from the German by Richard Massie, "Christ Jesus Lay in Death's Strong Bands," in *The United Methodist Hymnal* #319. Emphasis mine.

9. Venantius Honorius Clementianus Fortunatus, "Hail Thee, Festival Day," in *The United Methodist Hymnal* #324. Emphasis mine.

10. Macarius, *Fifty Spiritual Homilies of Saint Macarius the Egyptian*, trans. A. J. Mason (n.p.: Aeterna, 2014), 93.

chapter six

1. Derek Webb, "A New Law," Spotify, *Mockingbird*, INO, 2005.

2. The Episcopal Church, *The Book of Common Prayer and Administration of the Sacraments and Other Rites and Ceremonies of the Church* (New York: Seabury Press, 1979), 872.

3. I should note that none of this is actually official United Methodist doctrine. Wesley's thoughts on the subject do not appear in the fifty-two standard sermons and are only briefly alluded to throughout his commentary, *Explanatory Notes upon the New Testament.* This complex system is not specifically noted as an article of faith or religion in the United Methodist Book of Discipline.

4. John Wesley, "Sermon 73, Of Hell," Wesley Center Online, accessed April 18, 2023, http://wesley.nnu.edu/john-wesley/the -sermons-of-john-wesley-1872-edition/sermon-73-of-hell/.

5. Jon M. Sweeney, *Inventing Hell* (Chicago: Acta, 2017), 80.

6. Never mind the fact that the Roman Empire *still existed* in what we today refer to as the Byzantine Empire, headquartered in Constantinople.

7. Sweeney, *Inventing Hell*, 162.

8. Dante Alighieri, *The Inferno*, trans. Henry Francis Cary (Chicago: Charles C. Thompson, [1866]), 149.

9. Dante, *Inferno*, 159.

10. Jerry Walls, *Purgatory* (New York: Oxford, 2012), 127. This

is my very different take on Jerry Walls's "Rapunzel and Gretel" thought experiment.

11. David Bentley Hart, *That All Shall Be Saved* (New Haven: Yale University Press, 2019), 149.

12. Hart, *That All Shall Be Saved*, 150.

chapter seven

1. David Bentley Hart, *The New Testament* (New Haven: Yale University Press, 2018), 52.

2. Ilaria L. E. Ramelli, *A Larger Hope?*, vol. 1, *Universal Salvation from Christian Beginnings to Julian of Norwich* (Eugene, OR: Cascade, 2019), 10–11.

3. Ramelli, *A Larger Hope?*, 11.

4. Ramelli, *A Larger Hope?*, 216–19.

5. Ramelli, *A Larger Hope?*, 11.

6. Based on a terrible interpretation of Rev. 21:21.

7. David Bentley Hart, *That All Shall Be Saved* (New Haven: Yale University Press, 2019), 116.

8. Clement of Alexandria, *Stromateis* 7.16.103.3, as quoted in Ramelli, *A Larger Hope?*, 29.

9. See David Bentley Hart, *The New Testament*, 53.

chapter eight

1. Apologies to my Orthodox friends out there. Growing up, my friends and I didn't even know you existed! Don't worry, though—I'm getting to you in the next chapter!

2. Neither of these characterizations represent an accurate or even gracious interpretation of Catholic doctrine.

3. John Paul II, *Catechism of the Catholic Church*, 2nd ed. (Washington, DC: United States Catholic Conference, 2011), article 12, section 3, paragraphs 1030–31, p. 261, https://www.usccb .org/sites/default/files/flipbooks/catechism/.

4. John Paul II, *Catechism of the Catholic Church*, article 12, section 3, paragraphs 1030–31, p. 262.

5. One wonders what might have happened if the seraph had kept his seat.

6. Benedict XVI, *Spe Salvi*, paragraph 47, November 30, 2007, https://www.vatican.va/content/benedict-xvi/en/encyclicals/documents/hf_ben-xvi_enc_20071130_spe-salvi.html.

7. Jerry L. Walls, *Purgatory* (New York: Oxford University Press, 2012), 53. This is also the reason that I reject the Roman Catholic view of Marian perfection and the immaculate conception. By somehow shielding Mary from original sin, God would be violating the very economy of grace that Jesus came to transform. By my logic, if God could do it for Mary, then it would be immoral for God not to do it for everybody.

8. Samuel Wells, "Refiner's Fire," sermon, December 10, 2006.

chapter nine

1. *Ethnos* is the Greek word that we translate as "nation" or "a people." This is where we get the term "ethnicity."

2. See Michael J. McClymond, *The Devil's Redemption* (Grand Rapids: Baker, 2020), 1024.

3. Ilaria L. E. Ramelli, *A Larger Hope?*, vol. 1, *Universal Salvation from Christian Beginnings to Julian of Norwich* (Eugene, OR: Cascade, 2019), 2.

4. See Ramelli, *A Larger Hope?*, 5.

chapter ten

1. C. S. Lewis, *The Great Divorce* (London: HarperCollins, 2015), 75.

2. Alistair Begg, sermon, "Amazing Love—Part 4," delivered June 17, 2001, at Parkside Church, Cleveland, Ohio, https://www.youtube.com/watch?v=tppmMDaK7nw&themeRefresh=1.

3. J. I. Packer, *Concise Theology* (Wheaton, IL: Crossway, 2020), 262–63.

4. Actually, Wesley was the inheritor of a theological tradition popularized by Jacob Arminius, a Dutch Reformed Church thinker who argued against Calvinist predestination. Wesley even published a magazine called *The Arminian* in his honor.

5. Ilaria L. E. Ramelli, *A Larger Hope?*, vol. 1, *Universal Salvation from Christian Beginnings to Julian of Norwich* (Eugene, OR: Cascade, 2019), 12.

6. Packer, *Concise Theology*, 262–63.

7. David Bentley Hart, *That All Shall Be Saved* (New Haven: Yale University Press, 2019), 177.

chapter eleven

1. *The Lord of the Rings: The Fellowship of the Ring, Extended Edition*, directed by Peter Jackson (New Line Cinema, 2001), Blu-ray.

2. David Bentley Hart, *The New Testament* (New Haven: Yale University Press, 2018).

3. David Bentley Hart, *That All Shall Be Saved* (New Haven: Yale University Press, 2019).

4. Ilaria L. E. Ramelli, *A Larger Hope?*, vol. 1, *Universal Salvation from Christian Beginnings to Julian of Norwich* (Eugene, OR: Cascade, 2019); Robin A. Parry and Ilaria L. E. Ramelli, *A Larger Hope?*, vol. 2, *Universal Salvation from the Reformation to the Nineteenth Century* (Eugene, OR: Cascade, 2019).

5. Jon M. Sweeney, *Inventing Hell* (Chicago: Acta, 2017).

6. Marc Thomas Shaw, *Dante's Road: The Journey Home for the Modern Soul* (Vestal, NY: Anamchara, 2019).

7. Alvin F. Kimel Jr., *Destined for Joy* (n.p.: The Works of George MacDonald, 2022), 223–75. There's actually quite a bit of controversy surrounding the Fifth Ecumenical Council (the Second Council of Constantinople) over whether the council

formally condemned Origen, a noted universalist of the early church, and whether the council formally condemned universalism itself as a heresy. Alvin Kimel offers a robust review of the council and its historical context and makes a compelling argument that, no, in fact, the church has not condemned either Origen or universalism in any official sense.